Canto is an imprint
titles, classic and mo
broad spectrum of su
interests. History, litera
archaeology, politics, religion, psychology,
philosophy and science are all represented
in Canto's specially selected list of titles,
which now offers some of the best and
most accessible of Cambridge publishing to
a wider readership.

The tall brown woman
face highly made up face
2nd ~~with brown~~ her a tall flower
flushed with pollen
The ~~cool~~ t
Hot except where the air
cools & shifts over the water
They lie beside the lake

Henrietta, the middle-aged
nymph
Margaret her whole days.
devoted to following the Louise
woodward case

Written by a prehistoric archaeologist, this book describes how man has extended his understanding of time and space far beyond that of his primate forebears through technology, social organization and, above all, his capacity for abstract thought. Prehistorians have shown that even Palaeolithic people had long outstripped their forebears in comprehending time and space; and social anthropologists have documented preindustrial societies in which people were fully aware of these dimensions but were severely restricted by their social and cultural worlds. Evidence for more expanded horizons first appeared with those civilizations which controlled extensive territories and recorded their history to some extent in writing. The transition to modern times was marked above all with the advance of geographical discovery culminating in the circumnavigation of the world and by the beginning of recorded history. Today, people are searching for explanations of what we know in terms of natural science. This involves looking beyond our world to outer space and seeking to understand our place in the cosmos.

# Space, Time and Man
## A Prehistorian's View

# Space, Time and Man
## A Prehistorian's View

### Grahame Clark

Emeritus Disney Professor of Archaeology
University of Cambridge

CAMBRIDGE
UNIVERSITY PRESS

Published by the Press Syndicate of the University of Cambridge
The Pitt Building, Trumpington Street, Cambridge CB2 1RP
40 West 20th Street, New York, NY 10011–4211, USA
10 Stamford Road, Oakleigh, Melbourne 3166, Australia

First published 1992
Canto edition 1994

Printed in Great Britain at the University Press, Cambridge

*A cataloguing in publication record for this book is available
from the British Library*

*Library of Congress cataloguing in publication data*

Clark, Grahame, 1907–
Space, time and man: a prehistorian's view / Grahame Clark.
p.    cm.
Includes bibliographical references and index.
ISBN 0 521 40065 1
1. Man, Prehistoric.    2. Civilization, Ancient.    3 Space and
time.    4. Social evolution.    I. Title.
GN739.C53    1992
930.1 – dc20    91-20491    CIP

ISBN 0 521 40065 1 hardback
ISBN 0 521 46762 4 paperback

# Contents

# Figures

# *Preface*

To describe and analyse the specific character which space and time assume in human experience is one of the most appealing and important tasks of an anthropological philosophy.

E. CASSIRER[1]

The famous philosopher Samuel Alexander once wrote[2] that all the vital problems of his subject depended on solving the question of what space and time are and how they are related to one another. The present book is not offered as a contribution to philosophy. It is devoted to reviewing people's perception of these basic dimensions in the course of their social evolution. It is thus primarily anthropological and historical in its concerns. It aims to show how people have achieved their humanity in part by attaining a fuller comprehension of their own place in time and space. In considering how men and women gained this fuller insight we have always to remember that they not only stemmed from but remain part of the animal kingdom. At the same time, in the course of their prehistory they have become a very special kind of animal. Indeed, this is the reason why in my view prehistory is worth intensive study. Since we have only attained a fuller understanding of our place in the universe in the course of the general development of our culture, it will be convenient to treat the matter historically, beginning with the emergence of *Homo sapiens* and culminating in communities cognizant of modern science. As I said at the end of my Hitchcock Lectures at Berkeley in 1969,[3] a more comprehensive grasp of the dimensions in which they lived has been of high adaptive value in the evolution of specifically human communities.

In writing a book of this kind, which I believe to be the first to deal with the topic of space and time over a span extending from animal ethology to modern cosmology, an author has to rely on work published by authorities in many fields beyond his own. If I have misinterpreted what they say I can only ask their indulgence and accept the blame. By the same token I must seek the indulgence of authors whose works I may to my loss have overlooked. In such a summary work it would be tedious to cite in detail all the sources on which I have in fact drawn. Instead I have merely listed in the notes at the end of the book those on which I have principally relied in the order in which I have used them. Apart from learning from their writings I owe much to the inspiration of having known a number of the authors personally. As an archaeologist with a special interest in economic prehistory I have long been concerned with animals as sources of food. I owe my interest in animal behaviour as such to Professor Thorpe, formerly a close neighbour. Geology, particularly Quaternary geology, is a subject in which I have necessarily been closely involved as a prehistorian, and the same applies to fossil man studied by human palaeontologists. At Cambridge my own subject, archaeology, has always been taught alongside social anthropology and I owe an immense debt to colleagues in that field, notably Meyer Fortes, Edmund Leach and E. Evans-Pritchard, not forgetting Donald Thomson who came to us for a brief period from Australia. From them and their writings I gained an abiding sense of the uses, economic and social, to which peoples living beyond the range of modern civilization have recently put space and time. A book to which I have frequently returned over the years has been *The Discovery of Time* by Stephen Toulmin and June Goodfield,[4] the former of whom visited my first excavation after the war, perhaps to see how an archaeologist went about conducting an experiment in time. Dennis Sciama, while he was a Fellow of Peterhouse, first fascinated me with cosmology and I can only hope he and his former pupils will forgive my very imperfect understanding of their books. Lastly, I have been encouraged to note the attention currently being directed by some of the younger Cambridge faculty, including Geoff Bailey,[5] the prehistorian, to the problems of time and space as these presented themselves to prehistoric man.

I would also like to thank all those who have helped in the production of the book, including my wife, Mollie, who has removed many defects from the text, and my subeditor, Margaret Deith.

# Acknowledgements

The publishers gratefully acknowledge permission to reproduce the following figures and illustrations:

Fig. 2, Aldine Atherton Inc.; figs. 3, 10, 11, 13, 15, 17, 37, 38, Oxford University Press; fig. 4, Professor R. G. Klein; fig. 9, The British Library; fig. 12, Professor Andrew Fleming and Antiquity Publications Ltd; fig. 14, Basil Blackwell; fig. 16, Mrs Dorita Thomson (photograph by Mr Donald Thomson); fig. 19, Souvenir Press Ltd; fig. 20, Methuen and Company; fig. 21, The Egyptian Museum, Cairo; fig. 23, Hirmer Verlag, Munich; fig. 26, Princeton University Press; fig. 27, The German Archaeological Institute in Rome; fig. 28, No. 9028F, Fototeca Unione at the American Academy in Rome; fig. 32, Harper and Row Publishers, Inc., and Hutchinson; fig. 35, Mr Daniel Schwartz, Zurich; fig. 36, Institute of History and Philology, Academia Sinica, Taiwan; fig. 42, The Science Photolibrary and Mr John Reader; fig. 45, The Trustees of the Science Museum; fig. 46, The Archives, California Institute of Technology; fig. 47 and the jacket, The Royal Astronomical Society; figs. 44, 48, The National Aeronautics and Space Administration, Washington, DC.

# I

# *From animal ecology to human history*

Whether any higher animals other than man are self-conscious is
a matter for speculation; but it is safe to say that man alone has an
idea of himself, which plays an important part in his behaviour.
LORD BRAIN[1]

We need to recognize from the outset that animals of any species
can only survive and reproduce thanks to their skills in exploiting their environments. As A. W. Thorpe,[2] founder Professor of
Animal Ethology at Cambridge, has reminded us, animals are
most plainly distinguished from plants by their capacity to
move. They owe their success in obtaining food and mates to
their ability to detect and secure them by traversing space and
appropriating them at the correct time. This is reflected not only
in their behaviour but also in their morphology. Animals that
move under their own power rather than being carried passively
by currents of air or water tend to assume elongated forms.
Further, their most acute sense organs and the orifices needed to
engulf their prey are most often situated in some kind of head
located in the forepart of their bodies.

The prime dimension in which animals move is that of space.
They are attuned to exploring their spatial environments in
order to locate the most favourable opportunities of satisfying
their appetites. On the other hand, as Thorpe went out of his
way to emphasize, animals also depend on memories of past
time. This is particularly evident from the movement of fish and
birds in the course of their breeding cycles. The development of
marking techniques, followed by the systematic recovery of
individuals, has provided a wealth of data. In the case of fish, we

1

know beyond doubt that salmon habitually return to spawn in the same rivers and sometimes even in the same parts of the river in which they had been born and where they spent their earliest years. It has been shown in the case of steelhead trout (*Salmo gairdneri*) that no fewer than 97.5 per cent returned to their parent stream and that another 2.1 per cent found their way to streams within four miles of that in which they began life. Moreover, they seem to have found their way back with little hesitation. Salmon have been timed to travel up to a hundred miles a day on their return run for spawning. Others were found to have maintained a daily average of around sixty miles over a period of twelve days. It is important to point out that these fish were returning to home waters for spawning after absences of from two to six years. For fish to have retraced their passages with such accuracy after spending their adult lives so far away suggests that they can only have done so as a result of memorizing their past experiences. Among the kinds of features in the environment to stimulate their memories were variations in the density and temperature of the water on their route, the precise nature of river beds, and such features as the sounds of waterfalls and rapids. Whatever clues they followed, it appears that fish returning to spawn in their original home waters relied on information gathered in the course of their previous experiences. In bringing these to bear on their breeding behaviour, salmon returning to spawn in home waters were not merely traversing great distances, but were also acting by reference to past time, their memories triggered directly by features of the external environment.

Even more remarkable experiments have been made on migrant birds. Many species in the northern hemisphere migrate south-west during the autumn and return in spring. During the day they are able to rely on the sun to maintain direction while operating some kind of internal check to compensate for diurnal changes. By night, on the other hand, they apparently rely on the stars for guidance, as one can see from the disorientation they suffer when the sky is overcast by cloud. Experiments have proved the ability of birds to traverse great distances and make landfall with notable precision. Shearwaters removed from Skokholm off the coast of Pembrokeshire and then transported to Cambridge in blacked-out boxes flew the return distance of 290 miles in six hours. Another consignment, this time flown from Boston Harbour in the United States of America, returned to their Skokholm burrows, a distance of some 3,050 miles, within thirteen days. Experiment has tested an even longer flight, in this case by Layson albatrosses, which traversed distances of some 4,120 miles from the Philippines to Midway Island in a matter of thirty-two days. Again, birds of the same species managed to fly from Whidbey Island, Washington, a distance of over 3,000 miles in only ten days. Although, as Thorpe admitted, knowledge of how such feats were accomplished is still incomplete, it seems fairly clear that the birds relied above all on observation of the sky. By attaching minute radio transmitters to migrating birds it has been possible to show that they flew astonishingly accurate courses. Thus, a Swanson's thrush observed in Wisconsin was shown to have travelled a distance of 450 miles, while actually taking a course totalling no more than 453 miles. Such a standard of economy would be the envy of many human navigators, even when allowance is made for the bird's experience of flying in the opposite direction.

Thorpe quotes a further instance, this time from the insect world, of the use of memory (in the sense of recollection of past experience) as a guide to movements in the present. The hunting wasp immobilizes caterpillars by stinging and then stores them in its burrows to feed the young from the eggs it will subsequently lay. The wasp will need to locate its original burrow in order to accommodate additional caterpillars. It does so by recognizing the relation of the burrow to familiar objects or markers. Experiment shows that it can do this even when the most obvious landmarks are removed. If a beehive is shifted at night, it is found that next morning the foragers will circle the hive long enough to learn a new set of landmarks as a guide to their return. Once more, Thorpe maintained, it is a case of profiting from past experience through memory activated by the environment.

Others have argued that some time clocks are innate. For instance, bees have been shown to be endowed with a sense of time which enables them to visit their best feeding-places at the most favourable junctures. When the bees have been drugged to speed up their metabolisms they arrive too early and when they have been cooled they are too late. In the case of cockroaches, the site of the internal clock has been located and it has been shown that their activities can be manipulated by the experimental removal and grafting of cells. Again, oysters, whose

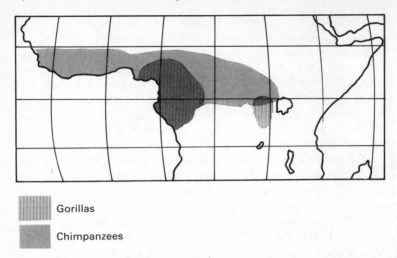

Gorillas

Chimpanzees

Figure 1 Map showing territories occupied by the man-like apes of equatorial Africa (After A. H. Schultz, *The Life of the Primates*, 1969)

temporal clocks are regulated by the tides, continue when they are transferred elsewhere to conform for a considerable time to the timetable prevailing in their native habitat. In either case the apprehension of time, whether innate or based on memory, is quite distinct from the conscious adjustments to time effected in human societies. Yet human beings still have biological clocks, even if they only become conscious of them when their routines are disturbed, for instance when they cross zones of longitude in the course of flight. The sense of disorientation we experience in jet lag is a reminder that, like other organisms, we have built-in clocks of which we are normally unaware, another reminder that we belong to the natural world.

The ethology of the non-human primates is of more relevance to human beings than that of other animals[3] for the very good reason that they are our closest living relatives, though the divergence of the hominid line took place some millions of years ago. So long as observers of primate behaviour confined their attention to animals subject to the artificial restraints and frustrations of captivity, their message to anthropologists remained limited and subject to critical discount. It is only since they addressed themselves to primates living at large in their

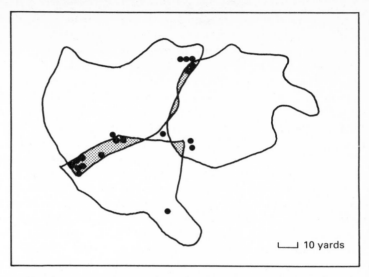

Figure 2 Adjacent, only marginally overlapping, territories of the South American Callicebus moloch monkeys, showing conflict areas in marginal zones (From Hans Kummer, *Primate Societies*, 1971)

natural environments and interacting with their fellows that primatologists have been able to contribute positively to the study of human behaviour. They have shown that non-human primates are narrowly restricted in relation to space.[4] By contrast with the ubiquity of human beings they are adapted to comparatively restricted ecological niches. Thus in present-day Africa, while humans are likely to occur in any zone capable of supporting life, the various species of non-human primate appear to be restricted to environments to which they are naturally adapted. While the rain forest shelters several species and the savannah two or three, the semi-desert supports only one. As Adolph Schultz[5] noted, those occupying territories with open vegetation need more extensive ones than forest dwellers (Figure 1). Terrestrial baboons, geladas and patas monkeys might wander some distance in their daily foraging, whereas most forest-dwelling species rarely move over more than one or two kilometres (Figure 2). In either case, they do not exceed the limits necessary for collecting sufficient food to satisfy their hunger. While apes and monkeys possess a remarkably accurate knowledge of the resources of their home environments, they are as a rule extremely averse to venturing beyond their accustomed territories so long as these supply them with sufficient food.[4,5] In other words their perception of space is limited to their biological needs, whereas men regard space as a dimension for meeting their socially and ultimately their ideological requirements. Again, where other primates depend on their own limbs to explore space, human beings have, in the course of time, invented artificial devices to assist them to explore increasingly remote zones of space and move about them with more accurate directional control and at an ever more rapid pace.

Observers of the non-human primates have also consistently noted that they possess only a most restricted awareness of past and future time, as well as lacking articulate speech. Although his studies were confined to captive animals, Wolfgang Köhler[6] was clear from his work on the mentality of apes that, despite any appearance to the contrary, these animals did not have a consciousness of time. Gaston Viaud[7] expressed it neatly when he wrote that chimpanzees 'are more or less trapped in the present'. And chimpanzees are not unique in this respect. Study of macaque monkeys has shown that 'their mental activities and processes ... are limited almost entirely to the present. Even when they are related to past experience, or refer to a very limited and immediate future, they appear always to be linked to sensory stimuli in the environmental present'. This restricted awareness of time is accompanied by a lack of articulate speech. The non-human primates are under no pressure to speak because they have little to talk about beyond what can be expressed by emotive grunts and cries. Conversely, it may well be asked in what a human conversation deprived of reference to past and future could consist. It is precisely men's and women's awareness that they exist in time that stamps them as human. Just as in the arboreal phase of primate existence the development of stereoscopic vision made possible the precise awareness of the three-dimensional space without which life in the trees would hardly have been possible, so in the case of human beings it was a sense of temporal perspective that made possible a way of life in which culture rather than mere instinct played a predominating role. That is what Ortega y Gasset meant when he exclaimed: 'Man has no nature; what he has is History'. It is hardly surprising that one of the ways in which he has used his powers of speech has been to transmit oral traditions about the way he lived in the past.

The conscious awareness that they exist in time which helps to distinguish human beings from other animals necessarily extends from the past to the future. Concern for the future is inherent in material culture, the medium on which archaeologists have mainly to rely in seeking to understand prehistory, and which is predicated upon the accumulation of capital. While many kinds of animal from birds to apes have been observed to use things in order to achieve immediate results, hominids alone have shown the foresight to make tools and other equipment for unspecified use in the future. From a remote stage in their prehistory they have shaped stone to serve immediate purposes, like detaching meat from the carcasses of dead animals. Yet for at least 2 million years they have displayed their humanity by making stone implements to standard, culturally defined and socially transmitted patterns intended for use on occasions yet to arise. In doing so they were investing against future contingencies. Frequently indeed they had to anticipate the manufacture of stone tools by securing, sometimes from a distance, the raw materials from which they were made. When they came to practise metallurgy, notably bronze-smithing, this frequently meant that they had to combine substances derived from more than one source, often from a distance. Another major investment against future contingencies involved the provision of devices to ease the movement of goods and people. On land these were not developed to any notable extent until the animals capable of drawing them had been domesticated. By sea it was another matter. Even prehistoric peoples equipped with elementary technologies showed themselves willing to devote arduous and often highly skilled labour to the production of sea-going craft designed for use on future occasions. It was the use of sea-going craft which opened up distant resources and for the first time made people aware of the extent of the world and of the place of their own communities within it. One may indeed conclude that the more advanced the material culture the greater the investment required to sustain, let alone improve it. The more insistent the needs and expectations the more pressing the necessity of anticipating the future. Conversely, the greater the requirements of the technology the greater the pressure on natural resources. It is no wonder that the vast increase in population and the greater impact made by modern technology should have led people to think more intently about the future of the environment itself, including even climatic and geological change.

One advantage of drawing upon animal and above all on primate ethology is that it reminds us that we are engaged in exploring aspects of behaviour which are in some respects common to all living creatures. Yet it is vitally important to be clear about one thing. Darwin, Huxley, Lyell, Lubbock and others have shown beyond cavil that our forebears have emerged in the course of the last few million years as species distinct from those which preceded them. One of their most important legacies is the question of what it is that nevertheless distinguishes human beings from their nearest primate relatives. A succinct answer is that supplied by Lord Brain in his book *Science and Man* and quoted at the head of this chapter.

Three years later in 1969 the Smithsonian Institution dedicated a symposium at Washington to the theme 'Man and Beast'.[8] Susanne Langer began by attacking those popular writers who specialized in 'applying ethnological terms metaphorically to animals'. Her strictures are hardly impaired by the practices of pre-scientific peoples. The ancient Egyptians, for instance, included animals among their deities and on occasion depicted them with human bodies and animal heads. Again, the totemic tribes of Australia were happy to trace their ancestry to animals or even plants. What Langer deplored was the damage to scientific discourse done by the writers of some popular works. We should not be misled by the undoubted fact that human beings may appear to behave like other animals in achieving biological ends. In reality the difference may be profound. Language may serve some of the same purposes as animal communication, but it differs in being conceptual and conveying a variety of meanings through the use of symbols designed to uphold values and proclaim differences inherited by virtue not of biology but of history. Human beings, according to Langer, owe their special position to existing at a level of awareness too intense to find adequate expression in immediate action: the world, the society to which they belong and their very sense of identity are all conceptual products. For Louis J. Halls, a fellow-contributor to the Washington symposium, great importance attaches to language as the medium for expressing self-conscious thought. Speech not merely establishes contact with other people but also conveys values as well as information and desires. The very use of language expresses the speaker's humanity and the essence of language is tense. A third contributor, Robin Fox, summed things up very clearly when he wrote, 'We are obviously part of nature, and in particular we are part of the animal world, and yet we are set apart from nature by the very fact of knowing we are part of it'.

In seeking the origins and early development of the conscious perception of space and time as dimensions, the obvious source is primitive man. The problem is where to find him. Our predecessors, still dazzled by the idea of evolution, had little room for doubt. The peoples encountered by ethnologists beyond the industrialized world were accepted as survivors of a primitive stage through which modern people had passed in the course of prehistoric times. It was assumed that ethnologists could gain direct access to primitive man by observing and interrogating such people. Yet in reality, as we have long recognized, the peoples studied by ethnologists lived on precisely the same level of time as their interrogators. They could not by any stretch of the imagination be accepted as representing pristine or primitive man. In many cases they had been modified in quite recent times by contact with traders and missionaries from the west and in others had almost certainly been influenced by earlier civilizations. Again, it should be remembered that the so-called primitives in fact stood at widely differing stages of development. For instance, when the inhabitants of the Pacific Islands and of much of the New World were technically still living in the Stone Age, others, notably in different parts of Africa, were already working iron. Again, while in many parts of the world the native peoples still lived in small, more or less egalitarian communities, many African and Polynesian peoples lived in societies to a greater or less degree stratified, with chiefs and in some cases with something like state organization. Furthermore, the anthropologists who recorded such peoples themselves had different interests and priorities. In many cases they made only passing references to perceptions of time and space. Evans-Pritchard's allocation of an entire chapter to this topic in his monograph on the Nuer was a rare exception. Yet there is a fair measure of agreement among anthropologists that the simpler communities living beyond the range of the modern industrial world invariably thought of space and time, not as abstract concepts, but in terms strictly relevant to their own ways of life.

Truly primitive people in fact lived a very long time ago. They can only be approached through a study of prehistory. Prehistorians are unable to interrogate or observe their subjects directly and truly primitive people were invariably preliterate. They can be approached only indirectly through a study of their archaeological structures and residues and these are likely to be most exiguous precisely for the early periods about which we would most like to be informed. Even so, the problem of interpreting archaeological data from remote periods is complicated by the fact that this has to be done in the light of more or less anachronistic analogies drawn from ethnology or history. The clues most likely to survive are those most remote from primitive peoples and in many instances reflect influences stemming from ancient civilizations. Nevertheless, despite its limitations, prehistoric archaeology offers the best prospect of spanning the gap between animal ethology and the historical records of the earliest civilizations.

The information recovered by ethnologists by observing peoples living until recently beyond the margins of modern civilization, when taken in conjunction with that inferred by archaeologists from the traces of prehistoric communities, nevertheless suggests that preliterate peoples had only a limited apprehension of space and time. As the French sociologist Emile Durkheim[9] once wrote, 'It is the rhythm of social life which is the basis of the category of time: the territory occupied by the society furnished the material category of space'. It follows that we may expect to find, as indeed we do, that the notions entertained by preliterate peoples about time and space related primarily to the nature of their economies and the structure of their societies.

The converse is no less true. If we aim to trace the development of ideas of space and time further, we need to turn to literate societies. Although we were right to begin with the smaller, relatively closed societies of the preliterate era, which reflect, however incompletely, the emergence of *Homo sapiens* as a distinct species of primate, in the long run the only point of doing so is to see what he has gone on to achieve in this regard since the beginning of written records. When people first became literate, around 5,000 years ago, they were enabled to control territories more extensive and more sharply defined than those occupied by preliterate tribes. Moreover, the territories of literate communities were polities, realms controlled by rulers or governing classes, which, unlike communities held together by kinship alone, were subject to a greater degree of specialization, not only in economic life but also in the services needed to meet the more complex requirements of states. The existence of documentary sources, however incomplete, in itself implies a notable increase in the evidence available for our present enquiry. Written historical sources give us a far better insight into their writers' appreciation of the dimensions of time and space than anything ethnologists could discover by questioning preliterate peoples or archaeologists could infer about their prehistoric ancestors from a study of their material remains. Moreover, the more advanced technologies practised by civilized peoples have produced a far richer body of archaeological evidence bearing on the extent to which they gave practical expression to their ideas about time and space.

It should therefore be possible, in later chapters, to present more detailed answers to the kind of questions raised in this book. It was during the historical period that the appreciation of space and time underwent such notable extensions. It will therefore be convenient to deal separately and in succession with preliterate societies, with civilized ones of the pre-scientific period and, finally, with those increasingly transformed by natural science.

The earlier millennia of literacy witnessed the emergence of a number of distinctive civilizations, all of which differed in several notable respects from those of prehistory. They occupied larger and more sharply defined territories. They were more highly stratified socially and in many cases they left useful written records behind them. They included the ancient civilizations of Egypt, the Near and Middle East and the Mediterranean basin, as well as medieval Christendom, which inherited the Graeco-Roman world, expanded further north in temperate Europe, established direct contact with China, discovered the Americas and circumnavigated the globe.

Historically the modern age began with the expansion of European civilization over the entire world. This resulted economically in the formation of a world market knitted together by means of communications which in turn were made possible by and at the same time facilitated the advance of natural science and the growth of modern industrial society.

Awareness of space, having comprehended the entire world, had still to be extended by means of telescopes far beyond what could be discerned by the naked eye, until, as a result of the work of radio astronomers, it came to encompass the universe as a whole. At the same time our understanding of time has ceased to be confined to what could be apprehended from written texts. It is only since the later eighteenth century that scientific concepts have assisted the building of a chronology based on the close study of material phenomena. Geologists and palaeontologists have between them made it possible to establish a sequence in the formation of the world and the appearance of successive forms of life, just as biologists have been able to produce a working hypothesis to account for this succession in the course of evolution. Similarly, archaeologists have been able to show by reference to successions of artefacts that in the course of prehistoric times people have increased their understanding of space and time while advancing their standard of living in a material sense, not necessarily as the means to that end. The very designation *Homo sapiens* suggests that men are distinguished among primates precisely in so far as they seek to advance their understanding as an end in itself. From the very moment human beings began to select objects from the natural world to turn them into useful implements, they had embarked on the dual process of enhancing their understanding as well as serving specific material needs. It may well be that cultural advances were in some cases triggered by chance, as happened with sports in respect of biological evolution. Yet the fact that persistent trends can often be discerned in the case of cultural advance argues that intelligence must have been a key factor. Prehistoric archaeology now allows us to discern the steps by which our own species has emerged from the primate stem and to see how it became progressively more human to the point at which the diverse civilizations developed that have left historical records behind them. From an early stage in his prehistory man has asked himself not only how the natural world operates, but why he himself is there. In particular there is evidence, notably in burials, that from quite early on members of *Homo sapiens* have concerned themselves with vistas of time extending beyond their own individual lives. Again, anthropologists have shown that even peoples whose ways of life may seem remote from those of civilized societies have nevertheless found it necessary to seek explanations for their own existence and that of their environments in terms of ancestors remote in time yet still embodied in myths and rituals.

# 2

*Space in preliterate societies*

One measure of the success of different species of animal is the range of environments in which they are able to flourish. In this respect human beings are supreme. In the course of prehistory they occupied or at least became aware of every environmental niche on earth.[1] Whereas other mammals are adapted to the conditions prevailing in a comparatively narrow range of environments, their cultural endowments allow people to exist in any part of the world. This may be seen by comparing their position with that of their nearest living relatives. The range of *Homo sapiens* not merely includes those of all other primates, but extends well beyond them. While at the present time in Africa the rain forest shelters several species of non-human primate, the savannah two or three and the semi-desert only one, human beings can be found in every one and extend in addition much further north. In this way the distribution of the non-human primates stands in marked contrast notably with the more pervasive distribution of ecologically polymorphic man.

Human groups did not acquire their ability to cope with a range of environments beyond those available to other primates in the course of purely biological evolution. Their expansion has been far too rapid to account for in terms of biology alone (Figure 3). The explanation must surely lie in their possession of an expanding culture. They have won their freedom from biotechnical constraints, in this as in other fields, by cultural means and by adopting the kind of behaviour needed to establish a foothold in an increasingly varied range of habitats. In particular, as archaeology so clearly shows, they have done so by devising the equipment and developing the know-how needed

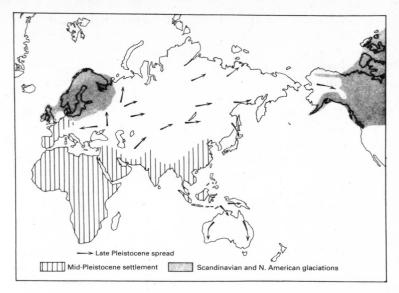

Figure 3  The worldwide expansion of human beings in the course of the Pleistocene (From P. R. S. Morey (ed.), *The Origins of Civilization*, 1979)

to explore and adapt to a range of habitats far beyond those available to other primates. It is true that they have only been able to do so because of the highly developed brain and nervous system which were parts of their biological endowment, but these were only able to operate effectively in the context of social development and indeed were themselves stimulated by cultural experience. Since people had effectively colonized almost the entire world before they started to record their experiences in writing, it is to prehistoric archaeology that we have to turn to supply the evidence we need.

During recent decades research has made it increasingly plain that the earliest stages in human evolution, cultural as well as biological, were enacted in territories to which all primates, including human beings, were then confined. Conversely, when people penetrated the cooler zones of the northern hemisphere in the course of later prehistory, they passed beyond the range of their fellow primates. Among the few exceptions were the relatively hardy macaque monkeys which expanded into southern Europe during phases of interglacial climate. When people reached the New World they entered a hemisphere in which the only other primates are today confined to South America. In the case of Australia there were no other primates on the continent.

The expansion and intensification of prehistoric research in the Soviet Union has recently shown that a decisive movement into northern territories was first effected by modern humans during the Late Pleistocene. This involved a vast territory extending south and east of the glaciation which centred on Scandinavia and still covered part of south-west Russia. It carried a sparse forest cover and had only a low snowfall. Conditions were ideal for mammoths and associated fauna which offered plenty of food to the hunters preying upon them. Soviet prehistorians have revealed many archaeological sites with Middle and Upper Palaeolithic artefacts north of latitude 65° and west of the Ural mountains.[2] East of the Urals many Upper Palaeolithic sites have been found well to the north of the Arctic Circle. These include the site of Berelekh, which has yielded a piece of bone with an engraving of a mammoth and is situated in the classic area for discoveries of frozen mammoths dating from the Ice Age.

The extensive regions of northern Russia first occupied during Late Glacial times were admittedly rich in food resources, notably in mammoths. At the same time they were excessively cold and could only have been occupied by people equipped to withstand the biting winds. Soviet prehistorians have recently substantiated the claim first advanced half a century ago by P. P. Ephimenko that groups of mammoth hunters were already building substantial dwellings during the Ice Age (Figure 4). Careful excavation of what at first appeared to be mere heaps of animal bones has shown them to mark the sites of elaborate structures, presumably draped by animal hides held in place by mammoth bones and ivory tusks. At Kostienki, Mezin and more recently at Mezhirich the outlines of dwellings were marked by mammoth skulls placed with their tooth sockets uppermost so as to provide footholds for roof supports. An impressive feature of the Mezhirich structure was that it was enclosed by stacks of mammoth mandibles and that the entrance was marked by overarching mammoth tusks. Beyond doubt the mammoth hunters of the Soviet Union built substantial houses to shelter from the extreme cold, much as the inhabitants of the circumpolar zone still do, though in a distinctive way. Since traces of

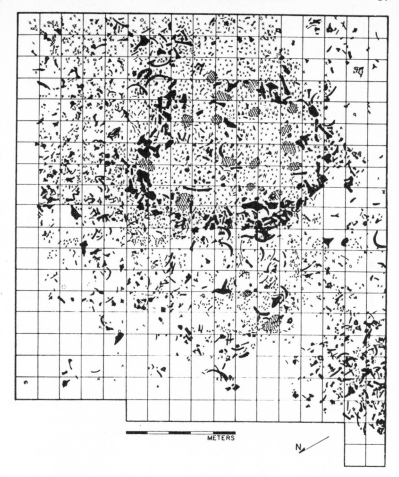

Figure 4 Plan of Late Glacial mammoth hunters' dwelling, Mezhirich, USSR

Mousterian (Middle Palaeolithic) as well as Upper Palaeolithic culture have been found north of latitude 65° on the west and up to around 61° on the east of the Ural mountains, it may be inferred that people had already occupied this zone in their Neanderthal form. It is hardly surprising that oval houses of similar kind should have been identified at Molodova in the

Ukraine, accompanied by remains of a Mousterian occupation of a type associated with Neanderthal man and dated by radiocarbon to around 44,000 years before the present.

Life in the far north during Late Glacial times called for windproof garments as well as warm houses. Clothing, being so much more perishable than dwellings, is likely to survive only under exceptional conditions. We therefore have to rely on sculptural representations. These point to the use of skin garments at least for wearing outside the shelter of dwellings. Finely eyed bone needles of the kind found in the Upper Palaeolithic Gravettian level at Mezin can, given the apparent absence of textiles at this time, almost certainly be interpreted as having been used for sewing animal skins. Again, the numerous bone beads found disposed over the bodies of well-preserved human skeletons at Sunghir, Vladimir, argues by analogy with Eskimo practice that the Gravettians had been buried in skin garments to which the beads had been attached. Lastly one might point to the well-known female figurines from Malta, Siberia, which are generally thought to represent people dressed in fur garments.

It appears that people first began to arrive in the New World during the Late Pleistocene, when sea-levels were sufficiently low to link Siberia and North America by the plain of Beringia. Like their favourite quarry, caribou and mammoth, they probably did so on foot. When they first arrived, perhaps some 20,000 or 25,000 years ago, access to the rich plains further south was barred by what was then a solid ice-sheet. It was only as this was breached by the parting of the Cordilleran and Laurentide ice-sheets around 12,000 years ago that the PalaeoIndians were able to press south. Archaeology shows that they fanned out rapidly, passing south of the Laurentide ice-sheet and eastwards to Newfoundland and New England and on the other hand skirting the Cordilleran sheet to spread as far west as California. The speed with which they occupied so large a part of North America is understandable in view of the fact that they encountered no significant competitors. What does call for remark is the fact that, if we may depend on radiocarbon determination for sites in the extreme south of South America, they traversed the western hemisphere from top to bottom in a few centuries, passing twice through a formidable sequence of ecological zones. This achievement alone demonstrates in an unmistakable way the advantages conferred by culture over biology.

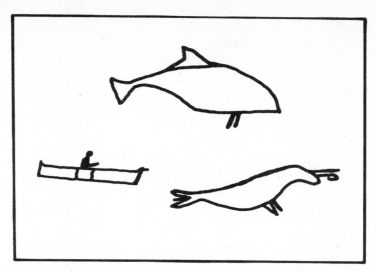

Figure 5  Rock engraving of man in skin boat with porpose and seal, Rödöy, Nordland, Norway (After E. Gjessing).

Another illustration documented by archaeology is the occupation of the circumpolar zone by prehistoric people, who displayed remarkable ingenuity in moving around, building shelters and securing food, clothing and fuel in one of the most desolate climates on earth. During the last 4,000 years the forebears of the Eskimo or Inuit developed a way of life which enabled them not only to survive but also to develop a culture which has captured the imagination of all those who have studied it. It is hard to know which to admire most, the ingenuity of their boats and dog-drawn sledges, the daring with which they constructed their houses or igloos from snow, the cut and style of their fur garments or the deftness and effectiveness of the gear they made to catch the fish, caribou and seals on which they depended for survival. The sheer aptness of their culture as a means of coping with an environment which has challenged and often defeated modern European explorers makes it all the sadder that, perhaps inevitably, they have fallen victim to the welfare dispensed by the functionaries of modern western society.

The contraction of the Scandinavian ice-sheet offered new

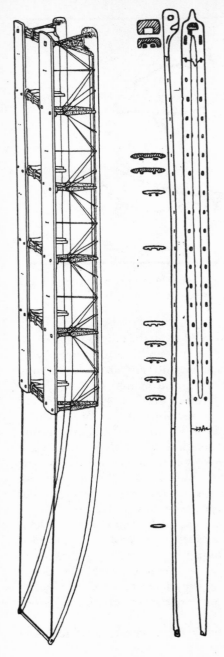

Figure 6 Stone Age sledge from Finland: (*upper*) reconstruction; (*lower*) wooden runner from Kuortane.

opportunities at the north European extremity of the circum-polar zone.[3] North of the mountain backbone of the Scandin-avian peninsula the coastal zone offered particularly productive opportunities for the intensive pursuit of fishing and the hunting of seals and whales. These chances could only be realized by developing sea-going boats and a variety of devices for catching and hunting (Figure 5). Although the Gulf Stream warmed the coast of Norway as far up as Finnmark, settlement during the winter called for the construction of substantial dwellings. These were made largely of turf reinforced by stone and their floors were excavated below ground level. They were set close to the sea and were grouped so as to house a number of families in order to provide crews. Although the food–quest shifted during the brief summer to hunting herbivores like reindeer, the sea provided the main resources for the early settlers of northern-most Scandinavia. South and east of the mountain backbone over much of Sweden, Finland and northern Russia, heavy snowfall offered a further opportunity to the early inhabitants. The use of skis and sledges turned a potential handicap into a notable advantage (Figure 6). Modern explorers in the Arctic who employ dog-teams to haul their sledges, and winter sports-men in the Alps might well reflect that the sliding devices they use for movement or enjoyment were originally invented 7,000 or 8,000 years ago to further the expansion of prehistoric peoples in northern Europe.

Another way in which preliterate people expanded their exploration of space was by the use of boats for crossing the open sea. When they first began to do so remains an open question. An obvious clue is offered by the passage of early man around 40,000 years ago from South-east Asia to Australia.[4, 5] Radio-carbon dates from a number of sites in Australia suggest that this occurred well back in the Pleistocene. Even if it is assumed, as seems highly probable, that the immigration occurred at a time when sea-levels were substantially lower than they are today, it must still be accepted that, as well as engaging in island-hopping, the Stone Age people faced the need to cross at least fifty miles of open sea. This means that they must have used floats or rafts, if not boats. Allowing for the possibility of accidental movements this need not necessarily imply planned navigation. It neverthe-less shows that the open sea was no certain barrier to movement for Palaeolithic man. It is not until much later in the Stone Age

that the evidence for navigation comes more sharply into focus.
Archaeology shows that by the sixth, if not the seventh,
millennium BC the island of Crete had been effectively colonized, and that Cyprus and other smaller islands in the Aegean and
the east Mediterranean were also occupied by Neolithic people.
In the course of the Bronze Age maritime traffic in the east
Mediterranean extending to Egypt and the Levant can be traced
with some clarity. By the middle of the second millennium BC,
by which time the Greeks had started to use writing, commercial
enterprise associated with the spread of Mycenaean styles
extended over a territory from south Italy to the Black Sea and
as far south as Egypt.

Meanwhile, there is evidence that sea-borne movements
extended from the west Mediterranean around the Atlantic
shore as far as the Baltic. The distribution of rock-cut and
megalithic tombs[6] associated with collective burial and a variety
of idols and rock engravings certainly points to an extension of
sea traffic (Figure 7). By the third millennium BC navigation was
sufficiently well developed to traverse the Bay of Biscay, extend
to Northern Ireland, south-west Scotland and the Northern Isles
and even reach the west Baltic. No traces have yet been found of
the vessels by which such voyages were accomplished. One
possibility is that skin boats were used. Certainly skin boats like
those recently employed in the circumpolar zone were used by
the Stone Age fishermen of western Norway. Moreover, it was
in such boats that holy men from Ireland are said to have found
refuge in the Faroes and in Iceland. Yet in view of what the
Polynesians were able to make with their stone adzes it can
hardly be argued that the megalithic tomb-builders of north-
western Europe would have been incapable of building substantial wooden boats. By the second millennium BC maritime
traffic in this region can be defined with more precision. The
recovery of hoards of bronzes off the coast of southern England
is one clue.[7] Those recovered by divers 500 m off Langdon Cliff
east of Dover harbour and again from a depth of 5 m or 6 m in the
sea bed some 3 km east of the bar at the mouth of the Salcombe
estuary, Devon, consist of forms characteristic of east and west
France. The circumstances under which they were found and the
fact that they were composed of objects originating from
disparate exotic sources argue that they represent the remains of
wrecks of vessels engaged in an extensive network of exchange.

Figure 7 Distribution of passage graves (After Glyn Daniel, *The Megalith Builders of Western Europe*, 1958)

The well-known hoard from the river Huelva flowing into the Gulf of Cadiz makes the same point even more effectively. It includes spearheads made in Britain and fibulae from the east Mediterranean, but pointedly excludes objects made in Iberia itself. Archaeology shows clearly enough that during the Bronze Age there was a brisk traffic by sea, not only in the Mediterranean, but also along the Atlantic seaboard, not to mention the North Sea and the Baltic. It is from this time that we have the first evidence for sea-going timber craft in western Europe. One group of vessels that may be cited consists of the remains of three boats from North Ferriby on the north bank of the Humber half-way up the east coast of England,[8] which according to

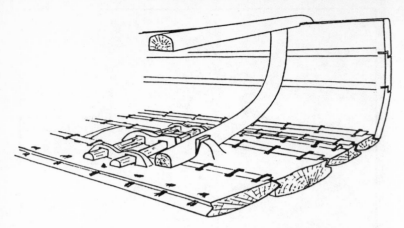

Figure 8  Sections of wooden boat from North Ferriby

radiocarbon dates belong to the latter part of the second millennium BC (1500–1250) (Figure 8). Although the Humber boats were relatively small, the better preserved one surviving only to the extent of some 52 feet (15.85 m), they were found to have been skilfully made from timber planks sewn together to present a carvel finish. In this respect they resemble the older and much larger cedar boat since recovered from the margin of the Great Pyramid of Gizeh and interpreted as the funeral boat of the IVth dynasty pharaoh Cheops.[9] The fact that boats made on the same principle are well known from India is a vivid reminder of the role of navigation in shrinking space.

By far the greatest scope for maritime exploration was offered by the Pacific Ocean.[10, 11] When this was first traversed by Europeans during the eighteenth century many of the Pacific Islands were found to have been already occupied. The fact that this must have been achieved by people still ignorant of metal made a deep impression on the European navigators. This was certainly the case with Captain Cook. On his second voyage to the Pacific (1772–5), which took him as far north as Hawaii, he particularly remarked the astonishing degree of uniformity displayed both culturally and racially by the inhabitants of islands scattered widely over an area covering nearly one-quarter of the circumference of the globe.

To a mariner this could only mean that the Polynesians had

spread rather rapidly from a common focus. Otherwise it would have been hard to account for the consistency of the cultural evidence brought home to England in the form of artefacts and illustrations made by the expedition's draughtsmen. Modern archaeology, backed by radiocarbon dates, points to the same conclusion. The ancestors of the Polynesians encountered by Captain Cook have been identified with the makers of a distinctive type of pottery, Lapita ware. This first appeared in the coastal zone of the Bismarck archipelago and neighbouring islands in Melanesia around the middle of the second millennium BC. Within the next thousand years this pottery had reached Tonga and Samoa in western Polynesia in the service of horticulturalists who made use of stone adzes. On the other hand, the particular types of tanged adzes and fishing gear carried over eastern and northern Polynesia did not appear until the first millennium AD. Radiocarbon dating has shown that the Polynesian culture spread with great rapidity as far east as Easter Island and as far north as the Hawaiian islands. The Polynesians owed their ability to spread so rapidly to their skills as boat-builders and navigators. Their mobility is also reflected in the history of their economy. The archaeological evidence shows that during the initial phase of movement they concentrated on resources immediately available, notably fish, turtles, sea-birds and porpoises. It was only as they settled down in the various island groups that the Polynesians, while retaining a keen interest in fish, came to rely primarily on horticulture and pigs, the main basis of subsistence of their forebears.

The Polynesians impressed Captain Cook above all by their skill and proficiency as boat-builders and their enterprise as navigators (Figure 9). They built their canoes from wooden planks sewn together and attached to timber frames. Although termed canoes, their vessels might be over 30 m in length and comprise a pair of hulls joined by platforms carrying substantial shelters. Such craft were capable of transporting over a hundred people. Moreover, they were highly manoeuvrable. Some were longer than *Endeavour* and were able to sail round it while it was on course as if it was still at anchor. Questioning the Polynesians showed that they often had a close knowledge of other islands, sometimes over considerable distances. The Tongans, for instance, were able to cite 153 different islands extending as far as Samoa over 500 miles away. The islanders were also found to

Figure 9  Tahitian double canoe, sketched by Captain Cook's draughts-man John Webber (From *The British Museum Yearbook 3, Captain Cook and the South Pacific*, 1979)

engage in return trips to many destinations. For instance, they made return voyages of up to 840 miles non-stop and others with only a single break up to as far as 1,400 miles. They gave many reasons for undertaking voyages. Some were economic. These included visits to better fishing grounds, relief from local famines and the replenishment of raw materials. Others were the outcome of rivalry between chiefs, which frequently led to raids or more serious attempts to establish domination over rivals. No doubt it was this which helps to explain the rich decoration carved on Polynesian canoes which caught the attention of Captain Cook's draughtsmen. In planning their voyages the Polynesians depended largely on experience gained on previous ventures. They had little in the way of equipment beyond the boats themselves. The 'sacred calabash' of the Hawaiians was no more than a bowl perforated by a row of holes through which stars could be sighted and recorded on notched sticks. As guides to the approach to dry land, close attention was paid to such signs as migratory birds, ocean swells and currents, odours wafted by the breeze, patches of seaweed and the glow of distant volcanoes. Of more general importance were the stars. In

Polynesia astronomy and navigation were almost identical.[12] Knowledge of the stars was constantly being gathered and applied at sea. To ensure that this was done most effectively the task was concentrated in the hands of a hierarchy of princely families. By accumulating knowledge these families were able to conceive of veritable sky domes which allowed them to infer their position at sea from observation of the sun and stars.

While the Polynesians were extending their knowledge of the Pacific, the Vikings of Scandinavia were active in the northern hemisphere.[13] From the Baltic they tapped the markets of Baghdad and Byzantium, following the rivers that flowed across Russia to the Caspian and Black Seas. In the south-west they passed through the Straits of Gibraltar to the Mediterranean, but it was in the north Atlantic that they voyaged furthest, opening up a knowledge of the circumpolar zone to Europeans and ultimately discovering the New World. How and why they did so and just where their voyages took them can only be inferred from archaeological evidence and the traditions embodied in the later sagas (Figure 10). Yet with all its uncertainties the story helps to confirm what preliterate people were able to accomplish despite possessing only limited navigational aids. When they first landed in Iceland between about 860 and 870 the Vikings had in fact been anticipated. According to the Irish monk Dicuil writing around 825, Celtic holy men had already reached the Faroes in quest of solitude, around 700 sailing in a small skin boat of two thwarts and from thence had paid the first visit to Iceland. Although something of this may have been known to the Norse, it seems that their own first visit to Iceland was involuntary. The subsequent voyage made by Flaki Vilgardsson, on the other hand, was fully intended, to judge from the fact that he took three ravens with him to help in making landfall. According to the story, the first to be released flew straight back home, the second returned to the ship, but the third pointed the way to Iceland. The prime objective was grazing. Within sixty years all the best land in Iceland had been taken up and pressure began to build up to seek additional land by fresh exploration. It was this that prompted Erik the Red, an outlaw from south-west Norway, to sail further west in the steps of Gunnbjorn, who some years before had been blown in that direction by storms. After an initial trial Erik returned to Greenland in 986. This time he took a fleet of ships and initiated the Norse phase of

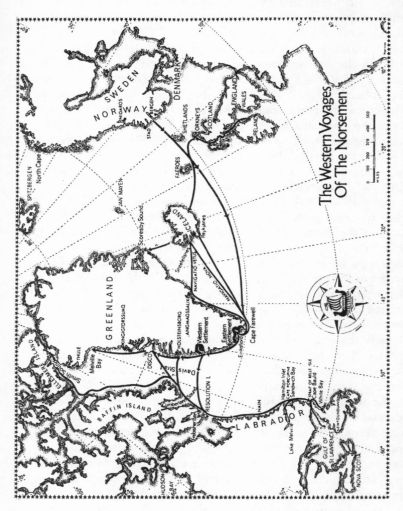

Figure 10  Map showing western voyages of the Norsemen (From Gwyn Jones, *A History of the Vikings*, 1985)

Greenland settlement that was to endure for around 500 years. After first occupying the territory later known as Julianehaab the Norsemen pressed further north. In addition they crossed the strait to what we know as Labrador. As often happened at this stage, their initial crossing was accidental, but purposive explorations were made in the opening decades of the eleventh century. The accounts of their voyages embodied in later sagas are confused, and valid archaeological evidence available at present only from the site at l'Anse aux Meadows at the northern tip of Newfoundland. Although this was only a transit station it is widely thought that the Vikings explored the coast of North America as far south as the Belle Isle Strait between Labrador and Newfoundland. The Norsemen were deterred in part by the unsuitability of the land for practising their own pastoral economy, but in large measure also by the unfriendly reception of the native inhabitants (*Skraeling*) whose forebears had entered North America from the west by way of Siberia, many thousands of years before. By the same token the Norse settlement of Greenland, though lasting half a millennium, reverted in the end to the Eskimo, who had learned how to adapt to the ecology of the region in the course of thousands of years. Between them the Polynesians and Vikings have shown how preliterate people possessed of even a modest level of technology were capable of experiencing and perceiving extensive vistas of space in the course of lengthy sea voyages by following clues, notably those offered by the stars.

Not only have human beings been able to move into zones extending well beyond those occupied by the several species of non-human primates by means of cultural adaptations, but individual groups of men have shown themselves able to command progressively more extensive territories. While non-human primates had to depend on resources more or less immediately at hand, archaeological evidence has shown that human beings have found ways of transcending the limitations of local resources. Prehistorians have been able to demonstrate this by the simple process of identifying the sources of materials used by successive populations. Thus the earliest stone tools recovered from Early Pleistocene levels in East Africa were found to have been made from materials available within a few miles. This distance was not much in excess of that covered by non-human primates. The Cape baboons of South Africa, for instance, obtained what they needed from territories only 5 or 10 square miles in extent. Prehistorians have been able to demonstrate a progressive expansion in the case of human groups. Analysis of the lithic material from Middle Palaeolithic levels[14] in the Aquitaine, for example, shows that Neanderthal groups still depended on materials drawn from relatively close at hand: between 65 and 98 per cent of their tools were made from materials available from within less than 5 km and between 2 and 20 per cent from between 5 and 20 km. The first breakthrough came with the appearance of people of modern type in Europe and the Middle East around 30,000 years ago. Even the pioneer excavators of the caves and rock-shelters of the Dordogne recognized that these Upper Palaeolithic people were obtaining mollusc shells from as far afield as the Mediterranean and even the Red Sea. More recent work on the cave deposits of south-west Germany[15] has confirmed that the Upper Palaeolithic inhabitants of the region were obtaining shells from as far afield as the Main and Paris basins and occasionally even from the Atlantic and Mediterranean around 600 km distant. In the Middle East it has been shown through systematic analysis of obsidian that Upper Palaeolithic people in Iraq and Iran[16] were using a kind only available from as far afield as Nemrut Dag on the west side of Lake Van in Anatolia more than 400 km distant as the crow flies. Evidence that materials were being obtained from distant sources is even more fully documented from Neolithic times, notably in respect of the flint and stone used to make the axe blades[17] that played a crucial role in the process of deforestation, but also in the case of the *Spondylus* shells which, from their source in the Aegean, found their way to peasant communities extending over south-eastern and central Europe to satisfy other social needs. In the case of the ensuing Bronze Age, its very existence depended on obtaining and diffusing copper and its rarer alloys arsenic and tin, often from remote sources.

At this point it is important to recognize a basic difference between human and non-human primates, one that intensified in the course of humanization. In the case of baboons it may be doubted whether they were even aware of territories beyond those needed for their survival as physical groups. So long as other species did not threaten them in this respect they tolerated them even to the extent of sharing the same watering place.

Human groups, on the other hand, had to satisfy cultural as well as merely biological needs. Indeed, they achieved their humanity by consciously belonging to social groups distinguished by sharing particular territories as well as particular languages, kinship systems, beliefs and styles, whether manifest in clothing, the treatment of hair, ornament or art. Such peoples recognized themselves as occupying specific territories. Although for much of the year the members of a tribe might be scattered in small groups, engaged on the primary task of acquiring food, they converged periodically to engage in a variety of ceremonial and social rituals such as the initiation of young men and the conduct of corroborees, the prime object of which was to transmit and maintain the culture of recognized tribal territories. The need to engage in social activities over and above those needed for physical survival is common to all human groups and embodies a notion of space beyond what was needed for merely physical survival.

The extent of social territories among the preliterate peoples of the recent past has been well studied by anthropologists. The Indians[18] of the Great Valley of California were found to have been organized in about fifty tribal groups aggregating in all some 15,000 to 20,000 people. The territories of individual tribes were rarely more than a couple of days' walk in any direction. Those of the Indians of the Pacific zone of Canada, as they were in 1725, extended no more than 75 or at most 325 miles across. Yet it needs to be emphasized that in these regions, as elsewhere in the world, preliterate peoples were not merely aware of neighbours but obtained artefacts and raw materials by exchange with these or even with more distant groups. For instance, the Indians of the Pacific coast obtained nephrite, as well as strings of centalia and serpula shell beads, from as far away as north Alaska and these are known to have circulated as far south as California. Whether the recipients had any clear idea where such exotic things came from is another matter. A classic study of the Walbiri aborigines of Central Australia[19] concluded that, although these people recognized many tribal groups beyond their own territories, their knowledge of them was so slight that they rarely knew more about them than their names and approximate territories. The only people to cross tribal boundaries as a rule were ceremonial messengers and the like. Materials might reach a territory from outside and be exchanged with others coming from different directions, whether supplies of red ochre, stone

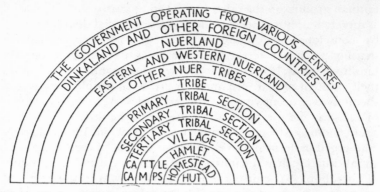

Figure 11 Spatial consciousness among the Nuer, extending from the hut to the government operating from various centres (From E. E. Evans-Pritchard, *The Nuer*, 1940)

axe-heads or spearheads of flaked stone, but their sources might be known in only the most general terms.

A noteworthy analysis of the perception of space entertained by a preliterate people is that published by Evans-Pritchard in respect of the Nuer,[20] a predominantly pastoral people occupying the swampy lands of the Upper Nile around the point where the Blue Nile heads south towards the equator (Figure 11). These people owed allegiance to a hierarchy of social groupings which occupied progressively wider territories from households to tribes, the largest unit with which the members felt obliged to combine to conduct raids on rivals, even if there was no obligation on individuals to take part. The Nuer as a whole felt themselves to be unique and to possess a distinctive culture of their own which contrasted with those of their neighbours, the Dinka and the Shiluk. The Nuer were aware of these but only as opponents in endemic warfare. Beyond their neighbours, the Nuer were at the time of Evans-Pritchard's research becoming uneasily aware of governmental authority exerted from beyond their ken.

By and large preliterate people thought of territory in structural terms. For the Nuer the tribe was the most effective unit in relation to other groups. The tribal territory set limits to the obligations of people as much as it gave them rights over a certain space. The extent of tribal territories was well known to their inhabitants and was frequently associated, as notably among the totemic aborigines of Australia, with the doings and movements of ancestors in the remote past. Tribal boundaries that might be marked by palisades or defensive works only appeared in the context of centralized polities among peoples who had attained or were close to attaining literacy. Within tribal territories space might be divided to accommodate constituent social groups. This was certainly the case among peoples whose economies were based on pastoral, horticultural or agricultural activities. The production, as opposed to the mere gathering, of food meant that land was more intensively used and, in the case of agriculturalists in particular, this led to the adoption of a sedentary mode of life. This in turn meant a sharper definition of ownership and property and a consequent stress on boundaries. Such a process was further intensified with the emergence of polities. Indeed, as will appear later, the growth of states during the historical period proved to be the main driving force behind the apprehension of space which led to man's occupation of the whole world and his exploration of outer space.

Evidence for the subdivision of land in prehistoric times has already been recovered by means of fieldwork and air photography. A good example is the recent recovery of evidence for the subdivision of land by the pioneers of settled farming on Dartmoor during the second millennium BC by means of reaves or low stone and earth walls (Figure 12).[21] Similar indications have recently been brought to light in other parts of England and Ireland. These have shown that prehistoric communities were laying out extensive networks over areas of up to 3,000 hectares and that these were oriented on common axes that ignored local topography: Neolithic Britons sometimes showed a similar grasp of space in laying out their sacred monuments. The Dorset Cursus, for example, extended over some 10 km and showed a similar disregard for local features. Other evidence that Neolithic and Bronze Age people had adopted abstract measures appears from a study of megalithic monuments in France and Britain. Professor Thom and his son have suggested that in laying out their stone circles these people employed a very precise unit of measurement, although these claims are by no means generally accepted.

By plotting the distributions of well-defined cultural fossils prehistorians have sometimes sought to define the territories of

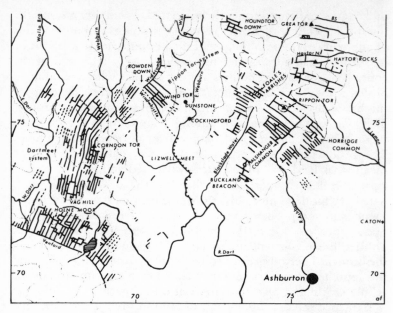

Figure 12 Co-axial field systems, east Dartmoor (From A. Fleming, *Antiquity* 196 (1987)

particular groups of Stone Age people.[22] Good instances of this relate to the definition of territories occupied by groups of Late Glacial and Postglacial hunter-fisher groups in northern Europe. Thus the Late Glacial reindeer hunters of this zone shared the use of tanged flint arrowheads, but three distinct styles have been recognized and these occur in three only marginally overlapping provinces: Ahrensburg points in Germany and the Netherlands, Bromme points in Denmark and southernmost Sweden and Swiderian ones focussed on Poland. Another example is provided by the different ways in which the Stone Age inhabitants of the coniferous forest zone of north Scandinavia, Finland and European Russia during later Postglacial times shared a taste for incorporating the forms of wild animals in their artefacts, but they did so, as the Finnish prehistorian Meinander has shown, in a variety of ways that coincided with well-defined geographical zones. While in Finland they preferred to shape animal heads on perforated stone tools, the inhabitants of northern and middle

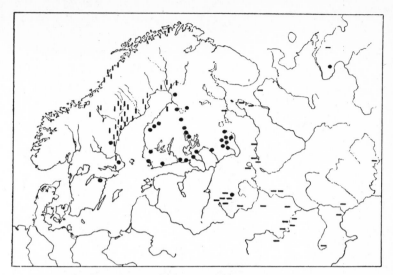

Figure 13  Map showing distribution of three kinds of animal sculpture from Scandinavia and northern Russia:
I    two-edged knives with elk-head terminals
●    perforated stone artefacts with animal heads
—    flints chipped into animal profiles

Sweden chose to carve the terminals of two-edged slate knives into elk heads and those of an extensive zone of Russia to delineate the profiles of different species by chipping flints (Figure 13). Here again the distributions were for the most part mutually exclusive, suggesting that they mirror the cultural choices of distinct tribal groups. Such exceptions as occur, notably the occurrence of Finnish types in middle Sweden, presumably reflect the kind of movement made possible by the use of skis and sledges during the winter months of snow cover.

As we have seen, one way in which prehistoric people differed from the non-human primates was in the degree to which they obtained raw materials from distant sources. In the civilizations known to history this was achieved by means of trade organized on a professional basis. Merchants grew rich by moving materials or the products of regional skills from territories where they were plentiful and cheap to ones in which they were scarce or absent and consequently more expensive. Although commerce

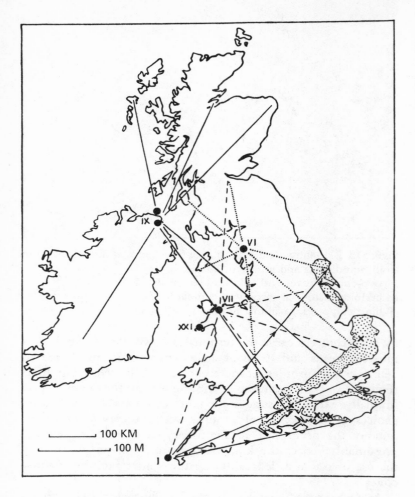

Figure 14  Map showing some elements in the flint and stone axe blade
traffic in the British Isles:
    chalk zones and sites of principal flint mines
    sites of chief stone axe factories and source: I west Cornwall, VI
Langdale, VII Graig Lwyd, IX Tievebulliagh, XXI Mynydd Rhiw
The maximal extension of products is indicated in each case by radial
lines.

on such a scale flourished only in relatively advanced societies, things were certainly moving, as we have shown, from far beyond the boundaries of the social groups they have been found with. A point to be emphasized is that the expansion in the zone of exchange during the last 30,000 years has from the outset been directed to a variety of social as well as to narrowly economic ends. It is significant that Upper Palaeolithic people imported molluscs from far beyond their own territories to satisfy aesthetic or magical needs. Even in the case of objects of such a functional character as stone axe blades, evidence from Neolithic Britain, based on intensive petrological examination of specimens from archaeological sites and a score or so of quarries, shows that their movements were the outcome of social rather than of purely economic needs (Figure 14). Thus blades made from porcellanite quarried at Tievebulliagh, Antrim, while clustering more densely in Northern Ireland, have also been found not only in western Scotland but as far south as the Lower Thames and Wessex. Plainly social as well as economic forces must have been at work. This is indeed confirmed by the concentration at Windmill Hill, Avebury, perhaps the most important cult centre in Neolithic Britain, of axe blades made of stone quarried at centres as far apart as Westmorland, North and South Wales and Cornwall. Whatever the forces responsible for such a pattern, its existence calls for a social rather than a merely economic explanation. This does not imply that Neolithic Britons perceived space as extending to the sources of materials they received from a distance any more than in the case of the Australian aborigines or the Pacific Coast Indians of British Columbia. It does, however, show that they must have been aware of receiving materials from regions beyond their immediate control.

It should be remembered that during the Stone Age movement over land could only be effected on foot. When they were not floated, heavy things like megalithic slabs or large timbers could only have been shifted by being dragged over the surface by gangs of people. Individuals can only have moved by running, walking, sliding or by water. Cattle were used for haulage in the course of farming, but domesticated horses did not appear in western Europe until the first millennium BC and then in the main to haul the war chariots or hearses of a chiefly class.

Apart from the timber causeways thrown over bogs and swamps, made-up roads did not exist. Such traffic as there was followed natural routes like the Jurassic zone which linked the Cotswolds to the Humber, or the Icknield Way that had guided movement along the chalk since Neolithic times from Wessex to East Anglia and during the historic period still served to define parish and county boundaries.

A direct clue to the mobility of preliterate peoples is given by their attainments as navigators and the measures they took to subdivide territory and plan large-scale monuments. At a more abstract level maps and charts provide a more incontrovertible insight into people's awareness of space. Edmund Leach went so far as to claim that 'the making and reading of two-dimensional maps is almost universal among mankind'. Yet most of the maps cited by ethnologists were in fact little more than so many jogs to the memory rather than symbolic portrayals of territory. Nevertheless, some were designed to recall landmarks in the mythological past. For instance, some of the patterns incised on Australian aboriginal shields have been interpreted as recalling the movements of ancestors in the dreamtime of long ago. Maps of the earth's surface intended to serve as guides to exploration had to wait until man had learned to write.

# 3

# Time in preliterate societies

Animals know only one world, the one which they perceive by experience, internal as well as external. Men alone have the faculty of conceiving the ideal, of adding something to the real.
EMILE DURKHEIM[1]

The ability to view time as a dimension, to look backwards, to view the present as the outcome of the past and at the same time as a platform for planning new developments in the future is one of the principal ways in which human beings display their identity as members of a distinct species of primate. It is of the essence of human societies, as opposed to those of other animal species, that they are constituted and motivated to a much greater extent by their inherited culture. Their attitudes and beliefs and the patterns of behaviour which stem from these have been widely recognized as having come from the past and, indeed, as deriving their validity by virtue of their antiquity. Human beings owe their distinctive character very largely to sharing social memories and upholding values inherited from the past.

Awareness of time as a vital dimension is recognized by anthropologists as a feature of the diverse human societies encountered beyond the frontiers of modern civilization. At what stage in prehistory this first emerged is problematic. One way in which people became conscious of time at a personal level must have come from an awareness of mortality. Among the non-human primates dead animals have no meaning. The corpses of dead individuals are simply discarded like faeces or the by-products of grooming. The dead have no significance for the

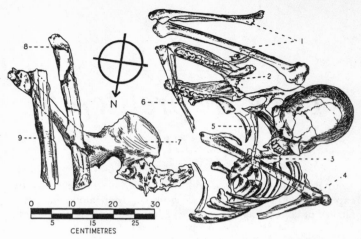

Figure 15  Nine burials on the terrace before the Mugharet es-Skhūl, Mount Carmel (From D. A. Garrod and D. M. Bate, *The Stone Age of Mount Carmel*, vol. 1, 1937)

living. The young gorilla reported to have clung to its dead leader when approached by men simply did not comprehend what had occurred. When people first began to ask themselves the meaning of death they posed a question to which priests and philosophers and not least their audiences have been addressing themselves ever since. At what stage in prehistory people became significantly aware of death as a personal fate and so paid special attention to the corpses of their fellows is hard to establish for certain, because the earliest hominid fossils in the form of fragmentary skulls generally occurred disembodied in geological deposits. The first signs which palaeontologists claim indicate that tool-making hominids may have paid any special attention to their dead relate to palaeoanthropic man and date from the Middle Pleistocene. Examination of the base of a skull of *Homo erectus sinanthropus* from Zhoukoudian[2] suggests that the *foramen magnum*, the hole at the base of the skull, may have been enlarged artificially to extract the brain in the way that the Melanesians have done in recent times, but it could be that we are really confronted by the effects of damage subsequent to the discarding of the skull. The earliest claim for formal burial relates to *Homo sapiens neanderthalensis*, an aberrant form of modern humans. Special mention may be made of two discoveries in south-west Asia, namely the cemetery excavated by Theodore McCown in front of the Mugharet es-Skhūl (Figure 15),[3] Mount Carmel, Palestine, and the burials at Shanidar[4] in north-east Iraq, uncovered by R. S. Solecki, one of which was of an individual who had apparently survived in crippled condition for some time before death. It was *Homo sapiens* who apparently began the practice that in subsequent ages provided archaeologists with some of their most precious clues to the unfolding of human culture.

Once people had become sufficiently aware that they existed in the context of time they naturally sought to account for their present situation in terms of the past. According to Frazer primitive man, by whom he meant preliterate people living beyond the margin of modern civilization, in fact went so far as to worship his ancestry.[5] What is certainly true is that such people were intensely aware of what they owed to their predecessors, starting with their own parents but extending back to periods of time far beyond anything of which they had any personal recollection. The myths they invented about ancestral doings were no mere mental exercise. On the contrary, they played a crucial role in validating the social structure and indeed the environment with which the society was familiar. This applied even to the Australian aborigines, who had been largely insulated from the outer world since they entered their continent around perhaps 40,000 or more years ago. According to Baldwin Spencer,[6] Gillen, Meggitt and their successors these people were convinced that the ancestors of each group shaped the configuration of the tribal territory, created the people and established their respective laws, customs and material cultures. They were interested in perpetuating myths about the 'dreamtime' primarily because of their bearing on their own societies and ways of life. By re-enacting the wanderings and doings of the ancestors of long ago, accompanied by rituals conforming precisely to those inherited from the ancestors, the aborigines sought to ensure and perpetuate their economies and the stability and validity of existing structures and patterns of behaviour. By in effect worshipping their ancestors they sought to invest their customary societies with the sanctions of antiquity and the support of supernatural forces.

Many examples could be quoted from Africa. A couple may

suffice. In his classic study of the Nuer, a Nilotic people of southern Sudan, Evans-Pritchard[7] observed that they displayed great interest in what he chose to term 'structural time'. Social status depended on the age-set in which young men had been initiated as fully adult members. Social institutions were shaped above all by the succession of generations. Although Nuer lineages covered only from between three and five generations, which meant that they spanned a bare century, even this was extremely valuable to the Nuer since, like all human communities, they owed their distinctive character to the fact that they had inherited their social structures, ways of life and ideology from the generations from which they were descended. Another instance may be quoted from the work of Meyer Fortes[8] in West Africa. In his study of the Tale Fortes argued that their social life was 'almost wholly organized by reference to relations of descent and kinship'. So central was this concern that a person's place in Tale society could only be determined in the light of precise genealogical knowledge. No wonder that among the Mututsi of Ruanda almost everyone could recite the names of his ancestors for six to eight generations. Among the groups studied by Fortes in West Africa it was common to be able to trace patrilineal lineages back ten or twelve generations. Filial piety led individuals to offer prayers and sacrifices at ancestral shrines. Doing so not merely assured them of their own place in the community; more importantly it helped to ensure the stability of the society to which they belonged. Among the Tallensi the lineage ancestors mediating through diviners were held to dispense justice and enforce the moral and religious values on which the social order rested. In more abstract terms, by increasing contact with the past through their ancestors these West African people discovered an extremely effective way of reinforcing the cultural dimension of their lives both individually and collectively. They were invoking, through appealing to their ancestors, the supreme sanction of the past.

The device of enlisting the sanction and validation of the ancestors was most effectively used by peoples who had invested most heavily in chieftainship as a way of promoting their success. This applied notably to the Polynesians, who maintained lengthy genealogies by word of mouth. These were zealously maintained and were used among other things to maintain and sanction the rights of conquest, discovery and ownership.

Among the Maori, members of the same tribe were related to one another by blood and these relationships were maintained in genealogies carried back to common ancestors. The Maori aimed indeed to trace their descent to members of the original crews to land their canoes in New Zealand. This led some New Zealand anthropologists to try and estimate the date of the original Maori colonization. Writing over seventy years ago Percy Smith[9] calculated that thirty-nine generations had elapsed since Kupe's legendary landing, from which he inferred that this must have occurred in the tenth century. By the same token we ought not to be surprised that it took a Maori chief, arguing before a New Zealand land commission in support of a tribal land claim, three days to complete a full recital of his thirty-four forebears, along with the names of collaterals and married partners, making a total of over 1,400 persons in all.

Because prehistoric societies were by definition unable to write, they left no written records and since they lived long ago they could not be observed directly, still less interrogated. It might be supposed therefore that there is no prospect of discovering how much such people were capable of drawing upon the past. Yet in fact this is far from being the case. The evidence on which archaeologists depend to trace the course of prehistory, notably the stratigraphic succession of assemblages of artefacts, in itself depends on the fact that these embody traditions handed on by successions of human societies over long periods of time. The traditions transmitted by human societies may relate to many generations or even centuries. The designs and modes of construction of houses, settlements and tombs, implements, weapons, personal ornaments and works of art were all part of the heritage, however much modified, passed from one generation to another. The transmission of cultural traditions even of the level encountered among preliterate peoples can only have been achieved through the uniquely human possession of articulate speech, just as the more complex cultures of more advanced societies depended on the written and in due course on the printed or electronically transmitted word. If prehistoric archaeology argues that the very process of cultural development was made possible by transmission from the past, enriched by successive innovations, common experience suggests that prehistoric people were themselves fully aware of what they owed to their parents and ancestors.

As we have already seen, one of the ways in which recent preliterate people preserved a knowledge of their forebears was by means of genealogy and this was more particularly so with the emergence of chieftainship. The same applied to the latest prehistoric peoples who featured, though dimly, in the earliest historical records.[10] This was true, for instance, of the proto-historic peoples of Britain and Ireland. They were frequently able to recite in their oral poetry the names of their rulers from long before they were able to write. The royal lines of Mercia and Wessex, though not written down until the latter part of the tenth century, were preserved in memory from as far back as the fifth and in the former case perhaps from the fourth century. Similarly, the succession of Welsh princes was remembered as far back as the fifth, although not committed to writing until the latter part of the tenth century, and the high kings of Ireland were held in memory as far back as around 400. The lines of rulers were remembered because the legitimacy of their dynasties was considered to reside in their antiquity.

The preliterate peoples studied by ethnologists were even more keenly aware of present time than they were of the past. It is important to stress that, while the non-human primates allocate their time in response to signals made by other members of the same biological group, human communities are constituted through much more complex inherited patterns of behaviour, patterns moreover which they understand in terms of their culture and which are subject to more drastic and sudden changes. Non-human primates respond instinctively, whereas people do so consciously by means of articulate speech. Anthropologists are agreed that the preliterate peoples they encountered were invariably aware of time, but equally that they were not concerned with it in the abstract. They took no account of time as something which flows at an even pace, regardless of human society.[11] On the contrary, modern preliterate people were concerned with time above all in respect of their own particular needs and requirements. Since preliterate people had no conception of abstract time they divided it according to local circumstances. This means that they followed widely differing indicators. For instance in his path-breaking study of *The Andaman Islanders*, whose appearance alongside Malinowski's *Argonauts of the Pacific* in 1922 laid the foundation for British social anthropo-

logy, Radcliffe-Brown observed that the people marked different times of the year by noting the succession of flowers
blooming at the various seasons. In doing so they concentrated
on the odoriferous plants on which the native bees depended for
their honey, a leading aspect of the Andaman Islanders' economy. This only serves to bring home the fact that, for such
people, time was important for scheduling their activities. While
this applied particularly to their economic activities it did so no
less to ones directed towards other social needs.

The importance of time for scheduling social activities applied
whatever the basis of subsistence might be. The Bushmen[12] who
lived by hunting and gathering distinguished the seasons primarily for their bearing on the food quest. Some groups distinguished three, others four seasons on the basis of rainfall.
When all had been passed, a new year began, but the people had
no conception of the year as a definite period of time. On this
account no one had any positive idea of his own age. He would
reckon it only by comparison with other members of the family.
Yet they were sufficiently concerned with the seasons themselves
to seek guidance from the stars about their onset. The Naron
group, for example, used the heliacal rising of the Pleiades as a
herald for the cold season. Not surprisingly the stars featured
prominently in their folklore and might be thought of as having
originally been animals or men before their transformation. The
Bushmen also observed the different phases of the moon and
divided the day in practice according to the position of the sun,
though there is no evidence that they had names for any fixed
divisions or parts of the day.

A detailed insight into the attention paid to the scheduling of
the food quest among the hunter-gatherers of Australia is
provided by Donald Thomson's study of the Wik Monkan tribe
of Cape York Peninsula in northern Queensland (Figure 16).[13]
His work brings out very clearly not only the complexity of
seasonal changes and their impact on the life of the people, but
also the way the people themselves recognized these both in
practice and in the terminology they employed. His account
shows how the aborigines responded to the variations in climate
stemming from the alternation of the north-western and south-
eastern monsoons. This affected the foods available at different
times of the year and also influenced both the movements of the
people and the types of shelter they built for different seasons.

Figure 16 Female of the Wik Monkan tribe of Cape York, Queensland, surrounded by the main vegetable harvest of the south-east monsoon season (From *Proceedings of the Prehistoric Society* (1939). Photograph by Donald Thomson, courtesy of Mrs Dorita Thomson)

Thomson was as impressed by the richness of the vocabulary they used to indicate seasonal variations in subsistence, settlement and technology as he was by their skill in scheduling movements and subsistence activities and not least by the manner in which they accommodated the ceremonial activities bearing on initiation, marriage and exchange, activities which enabled social groups to be maintained at a higher level of awareness than was needed for bare subsistence. From the New World one might quote from the early observations made by Father Chrétien Leclerc on the Micmac Indians of eastern Canada.[14] These people divided their calendar in terms of the condition of their most significant food resources:

Spring (*panian*) Leaves sprout, geese appear, fawns develop in wombs of moose, seals bear young.

Summer (*nob*) Salmon run upstream, geese shed feathers.

Autumn (*taouk*) Waterfowl move south.

Winter (*kesik*) Cold, snow, bears hibernate in trees.

Much the same applied to pastoralists. In his study of the Nuer of the southern Sudan, Evans-Pritchard showed how their social life and culture revolved around their observation of seasonal changes (Figure 17). Their affairs were regulated by ecology. They paid especially close attention to changes in the weather, notably in relation to rainfall and wind direction. The onset of persistent northerly winds served to mark the transition from the season of rain to that of drought. This in turn indicated a shift from village settlements to life in camps, together with a move from horticulture to hunting, fishing and gathering. Particular care was taken to observe the movements, growth and maturation of the animals and plants on which the people depended for food and for many of the raw materials needed for housing and material culture. They also looked to the heavenly bodies. They had names for each of the lunar months and distinguished the passing of day and night by observing the angle of the sun and watching the course of stars after sunset. It was into such ecological cycles that the Nuer fitted the patterns of their settlement, subsistence and social rituals. The keenness with which they observed the niceties of ecological change is reflected in the vocabularies related to the scheduling of their activities. It is of the essence of ecological time that it is cyclical. Year by year economic and social activities were geared to the repeated cycles displayed by natural phenomena.

Horticulturalists were even more closely tied to the seasons and depended for success on the close observation of ecological change. Raymond Firth[15] brought this out admirably in his study of the inhabitants of the small island of Tikopia situated east of the Solomon Islands in the Polynesian fringe of Melanesia. The islanders, he found, had no concept of time in the abstract as something to be measured in units, mathematically divisible and inexorably fleeting. Their concern was rather with the time needed to accomplish practical tasks such as converting raw materials into a meal, walking across the island, paddling the length of the reef and returning, sweeping the bay with a seine net or executing a number of dances. Leo Austin's account[16] of

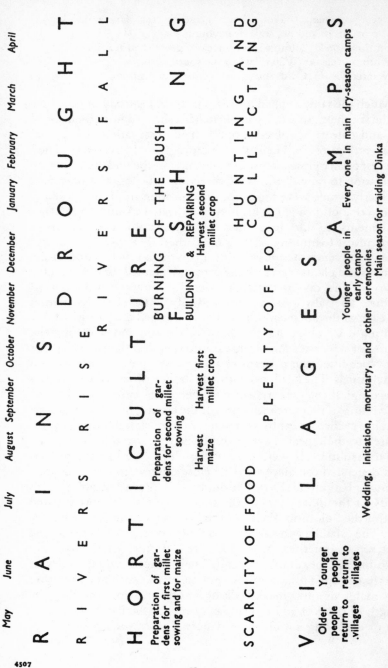

Figure 17 The scheduling of subsistence patterns, settlement and social life among the Nuer of the Upper Nile as observed by Evans-Pritchard between 1930 and 1936 (From E. E. Evans-Pritchard, *The Nuer*, 1940)

the way the Trobriand Islanders, among whom he spent some years as a magistrate, scheduled their activities is particularly interesting, especially the way the islanders managed to keep their all-important gardening calendars in phase with solar years, despite the fact that they lapsed into some disarray. Austin found that the islanders relied on the observation of certain stars to bring their calendars into line with solar years. In particular they depended on observing the heliacal rising of certain stars and constellations. Another point of interest is that the Trobriand Islanders, like the Polynesian seafarers, relied on specialists to keep watch on the stars. Garden magicians played much the same role as crew members charged with this special responsibility.

How far and at what stage preliterate people programmed their lives by observing timetables during their prehistoric phase can hardly be established by direct observation, still less by interrogation. Archaeology can help to only a limited extent. This applies particularly to the economic dimension. If prehistorians approach archaeological data in terms of palaeoecology they can sometimes recover significant information. Indeed, something has already been done to reveal the patterns of land occupation and subsistence as far back as Palaeolithic times. This patterning plainly implies that natural resources were exploited seasonally to support communities. The very success of prehistoric people occupying different zones and practising different economies suggests that they must have followed specific programmes. Again, the close comparability of the patterns inferred from food residues argues that communities sharing the same culture must have been capable of classifying and transmitting the data they encountered by means of language which took close account of the environment and of the methods used to exploit it.

A direct insight into prehistoric farming practices in Greece at the close of the prehistoric period is that provided by the earliest European poet whose writings have come down to us. During the Archaic period in Greece the poet Hesiod, a native of Boeotia, told how the prudent husbandman planned his work in accordance with the seasons.[17] He relied above all on observation of the heavenly bodies, but he also sought guidance from the plants and animals of his environment. When the Pleiades began to rise and the snails to climb up plants to escape the heat, he knew that he ought to have completed digging up his vineyards. When they were fully risen it was time to begin harvesting his grain. Their setting was a signal to plough his fields and bring the agricultural year to a close. The rise of Orion was a sign to thresh and store his grain, and its appearance an indication that his grapes should be gathered. Wine was considered to be at its best around the time of the heliacal rising of the Dog-star, which was also marked by the chatter of the cicada and the blooming of scolymus. The heavens also gave clues to mariners. The best time to go sailing was around fifty days after the solstice. When the Pleiades plunged into the ocean around the end of October, it was time to haul boats ashore. The trees also afforded useful hints. Sailors willing to take risks could undertake voyages in springtime when the first leaves appeared on the topmost shoots of the fig tree. Similarly, when trees shed their foliage and ceased to sprout, the farmer was reminded that it was time to fell timber and prepare it for making the ploughs and waggons needed for the coming year. Further clues were provided by the migrations of birds. The passage of cranes from their nesting places in Thrace, Macedonia and Scythia on the way to Cyrenaica, Egypt and Abyssinia marked the approach of winter and pointed to the need to press ahead with sowing. For those who delayed until the winter solstice the best hope was for rain to fall within days of the cuckoo breaking into song. The arrival of the swallow marked the approach of spring and served as a reminder to prune the vines. The theme of Hesiod's poem was to show how the husbandman could ensure success by careful observation of seasonal change. For defining the seasons which formed a background to his social and religious as well as to the economic activities with which Hesiod was concerned, it was necessary above all for him to keep a watch on the movements of the heavenly bodies.

An outstanding instance of the preoccupation of people on the verge of literate civilization with astronomy is provided by the Maya people of Mesoamerica between the fourth and the sixteenth centuries AD.[18] Although still practising a Stone Age technology, these people had developed a complex society focussed on elaborate ceremonial centres (Figure 18). The prime purpose of the astronomer-priests who officiated at these centres was to ensure the continuity of time and regulate the principal activities of their society. To this end they devised elaborate

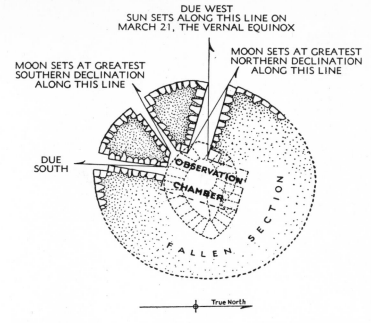

Figure 18  Maya observatory, Chichén Itzá, Yucatán, Mexico

calendars designed to ensure that the proper ceremonies were performed at the correct times. Knowledge of the astronomy that underlay them has come down to us largely through the codices or hieroglyphic manuscripts now preserved in European centres and originally made of *Ficus catonifolia* bark reduced to a pulp and held together by a natural gum. Maya astronomy was based on the systematic observation of such things as the waxing and waning of the moon as well as eclipses and the synodical revolution of the planet Venus. Lines of sight were taken through key points on ceremonial structures extending to distant features of the landscape, as well as from ones especially designed for the purpose. Although deploying only primitive means, the Maya attained a high degree of accuracy as a result of sustained observation. Thus they arrived at a duration of 365.2420 days for the solar year by comparison with the modern measurement of 365.2422 or the 365.2425 of the Gregorian calendar. Again, although differing slightly more with respect to the synodical

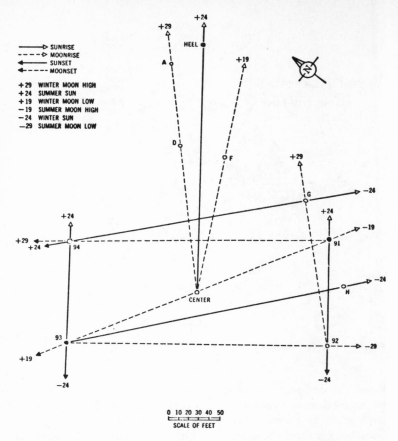

Figure 19 Schematic plan of Stonehenge showing astronomical alignments proposed by Gerald Hawkins, 1965 (From Gerald S. Hawkins,
*Stonehenge Decoded*, 1965)

revolution of Venus, coming up with 584 days against the
583.92 days of modern astronomers, the Maya were aware
that their determination was too high and devised a correc-
tion.

The extent of prehistoric navigation touched upon in the last
chapter makes it virtually certain that beyond sight of land the
Neolithic and Bronze Age Europeans relied on observing the
heavenly bodies to establish the positions of their boats. It is
likely that they also relied on them to regulate their schedules for

the raising of food and the conduct of social rituals. Evidence that they observed the sun, moon and certain stars with some care is suggested by the layout of some of their more impressive monuments. It is widely agreed that the eighteenth-century British antiquary William Stukeley was right in claiming that Stonehenge[19] had been aligned broadly on midsummer sunrise. Indeed, by noting that the axis on which Stonehenge had been planned differed marginally from that observed by modern astronomers and taking account of the annual shift in the obliquity of the sun's orbit set out in tables issued in 1863, the Astronomer Royal of the day, Sir Norman Lockyer, attempted to calculate the precise age of the monument in terms of our own solar calendar. The date he arrived at, 1680 ± 200 BC, would have been 1840 ± 275 BC had a more modern table been available to him. This at first appeared to be strikingly confirmed by the radiocarbon date of 3798 ± 200 years before the present obtained from a sample from one of the holes of the Aubrey circle belonging to the first phase at Stonehenge, though the agreement is rather less impressive when the radiocarbon date is calibrated against our own calendar. More recently an American astronomer, Gerald S. Hawkins,[20] has claimed, mainly on the basis of axes drawn through the corners of the rectangle formed by the two station stones 91 and 93 and the sites of two others (92 and 94) marked by so-called round barrows, that the first phase of Stonehenge could have served as a giant computer for regulating seasonal activities and forecasting events like eclipses of the sun and moon (Figure 19). On the other hand Hawkins was himself at pains to emphasize that the anthropological explanation for a monument like Stonehenge, a structure which must have involved a heavy investment in time and labour resumed on at least two occasions, when first the bluestone and later the sarsen circles were erected, and which served no obviously useful purpose, remains a matter for speculation. Few people would accept that its sole purpose was to provide an observatory for ensuring that the round of social activities was effectively linked with changes in the course of the solar year. This could after all have been achieved quite adequately by ramming a few sticks into the subsoil. Again, although the larger monument of the same general kind at Avebury has been assiduously tested, no significant alignments have been claimed to exist between its stone uprights and the sun or any other of the heavenly bodies. On the other hand, it is true that the late Professor Thom and his son[21] have devoted detailed attention to a large series of megalithic tombs and circles in the British Isles, Ireland and France and claim to have found repeated evidence that these monuments have been significantly aligned.

In seeking to evaluate such claims archaeologists have to take account of two main considerations. To begin with they have to decide whether the fact that astronomers and engineers equipped with modern mathematics are able to detect significant alignments in stone monuments, of which few of the components can be assumed to occupy their original positions, can safely be used to throw certain light on the considerations that may have guided the prehistoric architects. Then, even more fundamentally, they have to ask themselves whether subsistence farmers would have gone to so much trouble to erect their monuments to accord with the position and movements of the heavenly bodies. Put another way, we need to ask ourselves whether prehistoric people would have engaged in speculations beyond what was relevant to their practical needs. Yet we have to accept that one of the principal ways in which human beings differ from other animals lies in the effort they put into matters over and beyond what is needed for their biological survival. Prehistorians have shown that they engaged in such activities far back in the Stone Age. We know for example that even Lower Palaeolithic man gave expression to aesthetic feelings in shaping his principal tool, the hand-axe. Again, the art applied to the ceilings and walls of caves and rock-shelters in the Upper Palaeolithic and not least to many of the antler and bone artefacts recovered from the infill of dwelling places provides ample and incontrovertible evidence that people created works of art which served no direct economic purpose. The question is whether they also engaged in intellectual pursuits for their own sake. Alexander Marshack,[22] on the basis of his examination under magnification of markings on the surface of artefacts made from antler and bone from Upper Palaeolithic deposits in France and Spain and from as far east as the Soviet Union, argues that they did. Again and again he has convinced himself that the markings are grouped in a way that mirrors the waxing and waning of the moon. Examination under the microscope indicates that the marks on any piece were not made at a single session, as one might expect if they were intended for decoration, but on the contrary had been made at intervals. The drawings and paintings of wild animals on the walls and ceilings of caves and rock-shelters and the engravings found on the objects of antler, bone and stone excavated from the deposits accumulated on their floors bear ample evidence of the stimulus Upper Palaeolithic people derived from their environment. The markings studied by Marshack show that as far back as the Aurignacian period – the first stage of the Upper Palaeolithic sequence in France, preceding the Gravettian and the Magdalenian – the cave dwellers were also taking notice of changes in the night sky that must have been only too familiar to them. A point to be noted is that such time-factored notation first appeared in the context of *Homo sapiens sapiens*. No trace has yet been found in connection with Neanderthal man.

However sceptical we may be about the conclusions of authors like Gerald Hawkins and the Thoms, it must surely be accepted that *Homo sapiens* by his very nature can hardly have restricted his thoughts to what was immediately necessary for his daily life. The scale and increasing rate of innovation documented in the archaeological record is in itself an unmistakable sign that his thoughts must have run ahead of what was immediately required. One ought on a priori grounds to be prepared to accept that prehistoric man engaged in astronomical speculation beyond what his circumstances required. William Stukeley's attribution of Stonehenge to the Druids, the learned men encountered by Julius Caesar, still retains its hold on the popular imagination despite the fact that it is based on what historically speaking is an absurd anachronism. The possibility remains that such structures may in fact have been erected under the supervision of men entrusted, like those among the seafarers of Polynesia or the gardeners of the Trobriand Islands, with the task of observing the heavens. At the very least it may be that in the planning of Stonehenge care was taken to use the movements of the heavenly bodies as pointers to the scheduling of social activities.

Once people had become aware of time sufficiently to be interested in their ancestors or in the programming of their daily life it was inevitable that they should have begun to envisage the future. Time was after all a dimension, which began long ago, existed in the present and could only be assumed to extend into the future. The future was implied in everything ethnologists were able to observe about the preliterate peoples they studied beyond the industrial world. This applied in particular to the initiation rituals by which individuals were finally incorporated into adult society. Such people were as aware that time stretched forward as that it did backward. One sign of this is the steps they took to discover what the future held for them. The systems of divination studied by Meyer Fortes in West Africa were aimed at avoiding danger rather than offering precise forecasts, but at least they show that people were aware of the future as something they expected to experience for themselves.

The archaeological record shows that a concern for the future extended far back in prehistory. Even the most primitive stone industries were intended to serve beyond the immediate present to meet unknown contingencies. With the adoption of settled life in later prehistory the scale of investment designed to meet future needs inevitably increased. Even though populations were sparse and people lived in small communities, the long barrows, henges and cursus monuments constructed in Neolithic times were meant to endure. Excavations at Stonehenge have shown that, like the great Christian cathedrals, the monument underwent a number of major structural changes in the course of the centuries. Initially it comprised the circle of Aubrey Holes and the surrounding penannular bank and ditch. Each of the following two phases was marked by the import of stones for uprights. During the second phase bluestones were imported from the Prescelly mountains of Pembrokeshire. The stones used for building the lintelled circle and horseshoe of the third phase were large sarsen stones that appear to have been dragged across the Vale of Pewsey from their source on the North Wiltshire downs. The megalithic chamber tombs[23] were another feature of Neolithic Britain designed for use over a period of time, in this case for receiving burials from successive generations. Again, the economy which made it possible to create such structures itself implied investment in the future. The practice of farming implied that people had to invest in order to obtain their daily bread. The task of land clearance, followed by cultivation of the soil, the sowing of seed, harvesting and storing the crops, and still more the persistent control of breeding to improve livestock, all involved taking thought for the future with the aim of securing better returns from the effort involved in husbandry. If Neolithic people were to profit from their economy and secure the surplus needed for the construction of their monuments they can only have done so by adhering to some kind of traditional calendar in order to keep in step with the changing seasons, and the most reliable way of ensuring this was to maintain a close watch on movements of the heavenly bodies.

Another way in which prehistoric man displayed his concern for the future was in the interest he showed in what might lie beyond death and in the care he took to deposit grave goods. Although Neanderthal man may have buried his dead, it was modern man who, during the Late Palaeolithic phase of his prehistory, first began to provide them with the kind of equipment they had valued in life. For instance the burials at Sunghir, Vladimir, near Moscow, excavated by Soviet prehistorians and dated to 23,060 ± 600 before the present in radiocarbon years had evidently been buried fully clothed in leather garments decorated by quantities of shell beads and secured at the neck by bone bodkins (Figure 20).[24] An adult man wore ivory bracelets on his upper arms and two boys were buried alongside large mammoth ivory spears. From Neolithic times the concern with death and the beyond is impressively displayed by the megalithic chamber tombs of Atlantic Europe and the west Baltic area. The heavy outlay involved in their construction was offset by the fact that they were intended to serve successive generations. In fact they can be regarded as monuments to the stability of social groups. Successive interments were accompanied by offerings of decorated pots, which presumably contained food and drink, as well as by ornaments, implements and weapons.

A similar preoccupation was reflected in the princely burials which began to appear in temperate Europe during the Bronze Age and reached a climax around the middle of the first millennium BC at the height of the pre-Roman Iron Age. A tomb recently explored by German prehistorians near the fortress of Hohenasperg on the Upper Danube may well serve as an example.[25] The princely status of the person interred is shown by the fact that his neck-ring, armlet and fibula were made of gold, as was also the braid on his shoes. The tomb itself was lined with textiles and contained the iron-shod four-wheeled waggon on which he had been borne on his final journey, together with the harness of the two horses used to haul it. The chieftain himself rested on a reclining couch or throne. His quiver and

Figure 20  Upper part of the Upper Palaeolithic burial at Sunghir near Vladimir, USSR, showing personal ornaments (From G. Clark, *The Identity of Man*, 1986)

arrows were suspended above, and a small bag contained his metal fish-hooks as well as toilet articles. Like a modern landowner, his hobbies evidently included hunting and fishing. A set of gold-lipped drinking horns pointed to his role as master of the feast and a bronze kettle mounted with lions of Greek workmanship showed that one way in which he had displayed his power was to acquire goods of foreign workmanship as well as to dispense lavish hospitality. By providing the dead man with all the possessions he needed to maintain his status after death and depriving themselves of so much treasure his people had done their best to ensure his continued well-being in the future.

A final example, likewise drawn from temperate Europe, this time from its protohistoric phase, is afforded by the ship-burials of the Vikings and Anglo-Saxons. In cemeteries like Valsgarde and Vendel in middle Sweden the dead Viking was laid to rest in his most treasured possession, his ship, his body placed astern on his bed and accompanied by his personal ornaments, weapons, helmet and suit of mail. The gear concerned with navigating the ship was placed in the forepart along with provisions for meals, including joints of meat and other food, drinking horns, cauldrons and cooking equipment. The cargo also included a number of useful animals, notably horses, cattle, sheep, pigs, dogs and a variety of birds ranging from hawks to cranes, geese and ducks. Such lavish provision for the future came to a more or less abrupt halt with the adoption of Christianity. From that time the bodies of Vikings were brought to church and buried in holy ground. Their future was committed to God rather than being assured by rituals. The provision for Vikings was matched in wealth by the treasures buried with the Anglo-Saxon ship at Sutton Hoo in east Suffolk,[26] which included massive gold ornaments inlaid with garnet and silver vessels, among them a great dish with the stamp of Anastasius, emperor of Byzantium. Taken together, ship-burials of this kind remind us forcibly of the sacrifices made by the living to ensure the well-being of the departed, in future time.

# 4

# Civilization and the
# expansion of space

The growth of people's awareness of space, or as we might say a
sense of geography, was largely a function of the growth in scale
of political units. As we have seen, so long as people lived in
tribal societies their comprehension of space was restricted to
very small territories. It was only with the emergence of civilized
states that notions of space underwent a marked expansion.
States not merely occupied more extended territories than tribes.
They were also more highly integrated, involved greater con-
centrations of power and as a result showed a marked propensity
to effect contacts with distant neighbours and in the long run to
expand at the expense of the weaker among them. This led to the
formation of empires which yet further enlarged spatial horizons. It was rivalry between such empires as much as anything
that fuelled geographical discovery and by the close of medieval
times had brought almost the entire world within the cognizance
of Europeans.

The process may be observed at an early stage in ancient
Egypt.[1] This makes a good point of departure, not merely
because the Egyptian civilization was one of the first to appear,
but because it so clearly stemmed from the coalescence of
smaller territorial units. Dynastic history began in Egypt when
Upper and Lower Egypt were amalgamated by King Menes (or
Narmer). This is symbolized by the fact that throughout the
Dynastic period the crown worn by Egyptian kings combined
the white cone-shaped crown of Upper with the red cap-like
headgear of Lower Egypt. To judge from the scenes depicted on
the famous stone palette of Narmer (Figure 21), the amalgama-
tion when it came involved a good deal of forceful subjugation.

Figure 21 The palette of Narmer, symbolizing the unification of ancient Egypt. On this face the king wears the crown of Upper Egypt. On the other, he is shown wearing that of Lower Egypt.

The king, pointedly wearing the crown of Upper Egypt, is shown smiting a defeated enemy with his club, while Horus triumphs over the subjugated marsh dwellers of the Delta. It is still uncertain how the country was organized before its political unification led to the beginning of Egyptian history, though recent opinion inclines to the view that a substantial degree of cultural homogeneity already existed during Predynastic times. There was a sound reason for this in geography. Population was concentrated in the narrow strip of fertile ground either side of the Nile, which itself allowed easy movement. The prevailing southerly wind enabled boats to sail upstream easily, whereas passage downstream could be made by merely following the current of the river. It is the ease with which men and goods could move up and down the Nile that accounts for a substantial degree of homogeneity in Egyptian culture. Vase paintings on Predynastic pottery depict boats propelled by numerous oarsmen and provided with central cabins. The fact that many of the standards on the prows of Predynastic boats compare with those used to denote the nomes of Dynastic Egypt suggests that similar divisions may have existed during the Predynastic period and may even reflect the discrete tribal divisions of earlier prehistoric times.

By far the most important equipment devised by the ancient Egyptians to overcome the problem of space was the boat. Some idea of what Predynastic boats were like is provided by illustrations painted on pottery and by wooden models made to furnish burials (Figure 22), but the most impressive embodiment of their skill as shipwrights is the cedar boat 147 feet (44.8 m) in length recently discovered at the foot of the pyramid erected in honour of the IVth dynasty king Cheops.[2] This great boat had been built by stitching together planks with cords threaded through slots cut in their thickness. In addition, the pyramid builders must have used flat barges to float the heavy blocks of stone used in their construction from the opposite east bank where they were quarried. By contrast, they had to rely for land transport on the tractive power of human beings and donkeys. Horses were not introduced from Asia until the advent of the Hyksos and even then were restricted to drawing war chariots. Although the ancient Egyptians were largely self-sufficient, they obtained raw materials from Sinai, Palestine, Syria and Lebanon as well as from the land of Punt, tentatively identified with Somaliland. From a military standpoint they were powerful

Figure 22 Predynastic Egyptian boats: (*lower*) oared boats with cabins; (*upper*) sail boat (After L. Casson, *Ships and Seamanship in the Ancient World*, 1971)

enough to conduct campaigns in south-west Asia and on occasion even reach the Euphrates and confront the Hittites. They were not only well aware of their neighbours in North Africa and south-west Asia but thanks to their ships they were well acquainted with the east Mediterranean. This is reflected in the Cretan artefacts and Cypriot copper excavated from Egyptian tombs.

The archaeological remains of the Harappan civilization[3] which occupied the Indus basin during the third and second millennia BC provide further evidence for long-distance movements at this time. The homogeneity of culture prevailing over a

Figure 23  Wall painting from the tomb of Rekhmere, Thebes, Egypt
(After Lord Taylour, *The Mycenaeans*, 1964)

territory greater than that of ancient Egypt suggests that boats
must have played an important role in the Indus basin itself.
There is also evidence for more distant contacts. The occurrence
of Harappan seals from sites in the Tigris–Euphrates basin and in
Bahrain argues for traffic by way of the Persian Gulf.

The Mediterranean basin was another region to show how
geographical horizons expanded with civilization. As we have
already seen, the use of boats had helped the Aegean islanders to
extend their geographical awareness even as early as Neolithic
times. By the late Bronze Age the Minoan Cretans had made
contact with Dynastic Egypt. There seems little doubt that their
mariners had discovered how to make use of the Etesian summer
winds that blow from the north and north-west to set course for
Egypt and return by way of Syria and Cyprus. Certainly
Minoan vases were buried in Egyptian tombs early in the second
millennium BC as well as appearing at the same period at Byblos
and the ancient Egyptians also obtained useful materials from
Crete including oil, olives, wine and timber. It is suggestive that
some of the ships engraved on Minoan seals seem to have been
rigged in Egyptian style. The importance of traffic with Crete is
underlined by the abundance in Egyptian tombs of pottery of
Mycenaean style. The link between Crete and Egypt is particularly well seen in wall paintings in the tomb of Rekhmere
(Figure 23),[4] vizier of Tuthmosis III (1504–1450 BC), which
depict what an Egyptian would probably have thought of as
Mycenaean tribute to Pharaoh. This comprised gold and silver
vessels that could have come from Crete or mainland Greece,
textiles and copper ingots of the ox-hide form typical of Cyprus.

It took the Greeks some time to emerge from the 'Dark Age' marked in the archaeological record by the disappearance of the Mycenaean style. On the other hand the widespread adoption of iron-working, the invention of the alphabet and the genesis of classical Greek art, literature and philosophy were accompanied by a notable geographical expansion.[5] One of the first things the Greeks did was to cross the Aegean Sea to Asia Minor and colonize the coastal zone. The cities they founded there in turn established colonies far and wide (Figure 24). The citizens of Miletus took the lead in establishing the ones on the shore of the Black Sea. The Cymeans entered the mid-Mediterranean, settling near Naples, and the Phocaeans ventured as far west as the south of France, where they founded Massilia. Meanwhile, in the Mediterranean Greek colonists had to contend with the Phoenicians,[6] who had begun the process slightly earlier. From their base in the Levant these people had already reached Malta, Sardinia and what is now Tunisia, as well as having passed through the Straits of Gibraltar to establish a colony at Gades. Even so, the Massilians managed to establish a Greek colony at Emporiae on the coast of Catalonia. Between them the Greeks and Phoenicians had effectively engulfed the Mediterranean centuries before the Romans had conquered Italy, let alone established their empire.

A further expansion of geographical knowledge among the Greeks is reflected in the writings of Herodotus, whose travels around the middle of the fifth century BC extended well beyond the Mediterranean and the Black Sea. Herodotus gained experience of the greater part of the Persian Empire and the hinterlands of the Black Sea as well as Egypt and Libya. Even so, his knowledge was strictly limited. He knew nothing of eastern Europe beyond the Danube, had only a vague idea of the rivers of south Russia and knew only the southern portion of the Caspian. To the south his knowledge of Africa extended only from Morocco to the Red Sea. He had a reasonably accurate idea of the shape of Arabia and of the course of the Tigris and Euphrates, but he had only a vague one of the Persian Gulf and knew only of the bare existence of the Indus. Fuller knowledge had to wait on the conquest of the Persian Empire by Alexander the Great in 332–323 BC. Although at a political level his empire broke up into a number of kingdoms, the early death of Alexander signalled the beginning of the Hellenistic age of which

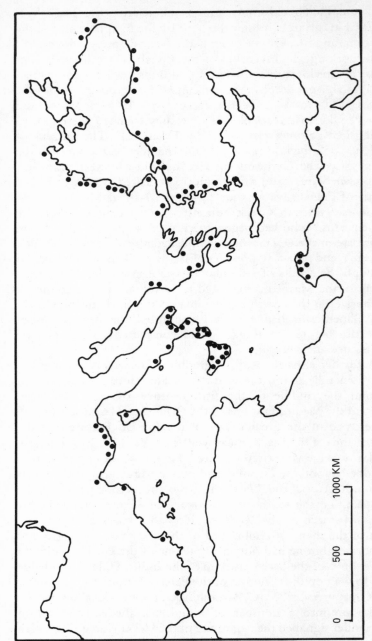

Figure 24  Map showing Greek colonization in the Mediterranean and the Black Sea: mid eighth to mid sixth century BC

1000 KM

500

0

his own foundation, Alexandria, was to remain the intellectual centre of the ancient world for something like a thousand years. It was through the Hellenistic world that Rome was in due course to absorb Greek knowledge and Christianity to emerge as a world religion.

The success of the Greeks as colonizers and traders reminds us that they relied on their astronomical knowledge to guide them at sea. Already in the sixth century BC Alexander of Miletus (611–546 BC), considered by the Greeks to have been the father of map-making, had envisaged the earth as a sphere. During the fourth century BC Eudoxus of Cnidos (408–355 BC), a pupil of Plato's, constructed a mechanism comprising a number of spheres to imitate the motions of the sun, moon and planets, contrived in such a way as to make it possible to forecast lunar and solar eclipses. Greek thinkers, indeed, sought to account rationally for the close dependence of navigators on astronomical observations, something which less sophisticated mariners knew well enough without recourse to theory. As the example of Pytheas, a contemporary of Alexander the Great, and a native of Massilia, well shows, the Greeks of his day were well able to determine latitudes by observing the duration of the longest days and noting the height of the sun at solstice. Although his own account has perished, it is known from other sources that Pytheas made extensive voyages in the direction of Britain. His claim to have circumnavigated Britain has been doubted, but it is widely accepted that he made extensive voyages along the Atlantic seaboard and reached at least as far north as the Isle of Man and north Germany.

The expansion of geographical knowledge from the Mediterranean to other parts of the world was accumulated and stored in the great library and museum at Alexandria. An early director, Eratosthenes (c. 275–194 BC), not only wrote works concerned with the measurement and disposition of space, but around 220 BC produced what is commonly held to have been the first scientific map of the world as it was then known. This took the form of an oval landmass surrounded by ocean. From west to east the world as it was then known to the Greeks extended from Britain to the Ganges. A northern limit was set by Thule, wherever this may have been. Scandinavia was excluded and only the southerly parts of Russia were covered. To the south, knowledge of Africa extended no further than what was known

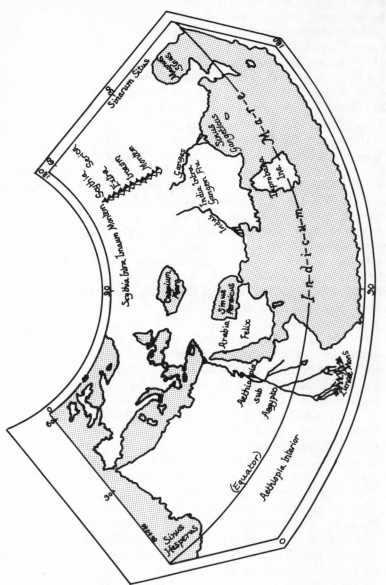

Figure 25 Ptolemy's world outline, from the Rome edition of 1490 (After Crone, *Maps and their Makers*, 1968)

to Herodotus and embraced only the northern zone from Morocco to the Red Sea. Further east Eratosthenes had a good idea of the Persian Gulf and his vision of the Indian Ocean extended to Ceylon even if it largely omitted peninsular India. It was at Alexandria also that Ptolemy (AD 90–168) compiled his guide to geography, which exerted a profound influence on the medieval geographers of the west. Ptolemy's work was in fact preserved for posterity by Arabic and Byzantine scholars but it was only when a Greek manuscript reached Florence from Byzantium and was translated into Latin in 1409 that it first influenced west European cartographers directly (Figure 25). Manuscript copies began to circulate in Europe during the opening decades of the fifteenth century, but it was not until the last quarter that printed editions first became available. One reason why Ptolemy made such an impact was that he imposed a grid of parallels of latitude and meridians of longitude on the globe and devised conical projections to produce flat outlines of land and sea as these were envisaged by the Romans and their contemporaries. Ironically, it was by placing the equator too far north and consequently making it too short that he encouraged Christopher Columbus to imagine that he could most readily reach the Far East by sailing west across the Atlantic.

At the height of their power the Romans not merely engulfed most of the territory of the Persian Empire and the spheres of the Greeks and Phoenicians in the Mediterranean, but expanded geographical knowledge further north and east. Furthermore, they went to some trouble to keep their own subjects informed about the extension of their territories. By the time of Trajan the empire had reached a stage at which it measured about 5,000 km from east to west and around half as much from north to south. It is true that a notable part of this extensive space was occupied by the Mediterranean, the Black Sea and the Atlantic coastal waters off western Europe. Yet it was precisely the sea which helped to promote the homogeneity of the empire. It made for much greater facility of movement in early times than dry land. As Moses Finley once remarked, a boat can carry cargoes from one end of the Mediterranean to another at less than the cost of transporting a similar load for a mere 75 miles (112 km) over land. Movement of the bulky and weighty materials on which the Roman economy depended over the distances we know to have been involved can only have been effected by boat (Figure

Figure 26  Roman cargo ship in full sail, carved on a sarcophagus of the second century AD (From Casson, *Ships and Seamanship in the Ancient World*, 1971)

26). Even the grain on which the Roman populace depended came largely from lands as distant as Spain, North Africa and Scythia. Again, supplies of oil and wine were in large measure drawn from Spain, Syria and the Aegean. It is equally true that many of the marbles used for public buildings and monuments were quarried in Spain, Numidia and Greece as well as in Italy itself. Furthermore, Roman technology depended to a notable extent on metals, many of which came from mines situated as far afield as Spain, the Balkans, Asia Minor and Cyprus.

Despite the importance of the sea for carrying heavy cargoes, the coherence of the empire in fact depended on the network of roads the Romans were at pains to develop as their territory expanded.[7,8] The planning and construction of roads played an integral part in the process of conquest and pacification. The movement of legions to mount offensives, quell disturbances or repel invaders depended on carefully planned and effectively maintained roads. An adequate network of roads also played an important part in operating the economy. The use of pack

Figure 27 Relief showing a dispatch carrier of the Roman *cursus publicus* in a light carriage drawn by three horses

Figure 28 Peutinger Table, showing regions around Rome. The table as a whole is over 22 feet (7 m) long and 13 inches (32 cm) deep. It provides a schematic picture of the Roman road system for travellers, giving distances between places and the facilities provided for travellers in respect of accommodation, relays of animals, etc.

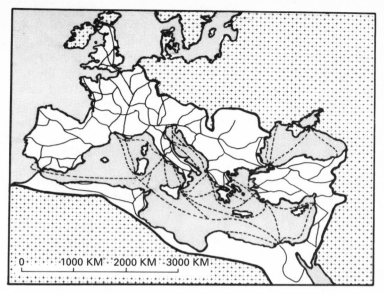

Figure 29 Map showing the communications network in the Roman Empire (areas outside the empire shown in stipple)

animals and ox-drawn waggons must have played a vital role in harvesting crops, spreading manure and not least in ensuring the distribution of manufactured products like pottery and textiles (Figure 27). Even more importantly roads played a crucial part in maintaining official control of the empire from Rome. The map of the empire prepared by Agrippa and after his death completed and put on public display by Augustus was to an important degree based on the road system. A good idea of the kind of information available to travellers is provided by the Peutinger Table which takes its name from a medieval owner (Figure 28). Travellers in Roman times did not carry maps but narrow rolls on which were inscribed the distances between staging points along the main routes. Stations were provided at intervals for changing horses, as well as rest-houses for those who used the route. Although the Imperial Post only reckoned as a rule to cover fifty miles a day, messengers were able in emergencies to travel more rapidly. The main thing to remember is that if by modern standards communications were extremely slow, at least they were sure for those concerned with public business.

The mere existence of such a system with its milestones and flow of traffic must have enhanced people's perception of the extent of the empire and of the degree to which its operations and security were supervised by official authority (Figure 29).

The sense of belonging to a polity of majestic proportions must have been enhanced by the widespread use and understanding of the Latin language. Archaeology shows that the engravings on Roman monuments were not only written in the same language but employed the same formulae. Again, it is significant that references to such matters as military accounts, pay-sheets and supplies inscribed on the wax tablets recently recovered from the fort of Chesterholm (Vindolanda)[9] on Hadrian's Wall were remarkably similar to those found inscribed on papyri from Egypt. The evidence of literature is even more impressive. Although many well-known authors were born in Italy, a substantial number came from the provinces. The south of Spain contributed the Senecas, father and son, as well as the poet Lucan, the agriculturalist Columella and the geographer Melas. A wide range of writers came from North Africa, from the novelist and orator Apuleius and the dramatist Terence to theologians like Sts Cyprian and Augustine. Other well-known classical authors came from Syria, and Yugoslavia contributed the poet Juvenal and the theologian Jerome.

The sense of belonging to an extensive and for long a growing empire was encouraged by its rulers. Julius Caesar not only conquered Gaul. He made sure of his enduring fame by describing his conquest in *De Bello Gallico*, one of the classics of Latin or indeed of western literature. At the same time he took practical steps to ensure that the Romans were made visually aware of the total extent of their empire. He commissioned Greek geographers to construct a map of the entire empire as it existed in his day and he took care to ensure that their work was displayed to enlighten the general public. His successor, the emperor Augustus, pursued the same policy by charging his son-in-law Agrippa with a similar enterprise. When Agrippa died in 12 BC the emperor made sure that the task was completed and the results displayed to the citizens at large on the Porticus Vipsanius in Rome. In seeking to involve their public in the growth of the empire Roman rulers were only following a precedent set in Greece. Already during the third century BC the Athenians had displayed maps of the known world as a way of keeping their citizens informed of their situation.

The traditional aim of Roman authority had been to extend the limits of the empire by military means followed up by administrative and cultural measures to ensure the incorporation of new territories within the Roman world. When Trajan became emperor in AD 98 he began by pursuing the same policy in annexing Armenia and Dacia, yet he found it politic to withdraw from southern Mesopotamia. In fact the Roman Empire had reached its zenith and it was left to his successor Hadrian to consolidate the frontiers. This he did by building the wall that bears his name to define and protect the province of Britain, as well as by constructing the *limes* between the Rhine and the Danube, the rivers that effectively defined the northern frontier of much of the empire. The Roman perception of space was by no means limited to the territories enclosed within the frontiers of the empire. The very construction of defences itself presupposes some knowledge of the neighbours against whom they were built. The military defences of the empire were very much the outcome of relations between Rome and its neighbours. During the reign of Augustus his stepson, Drusus, had campaigned in Free Germany as far east as the Elbe. Again, Hadrian's successor, Antoninus Pius, campaigned in Scotland and even erected the turf wall that bears his name and for some forty years formed a frontier linking the Firths of Forth and Clyde, some distance north of that for which the Romans ultimately settled. Like any other people defending an extensive territory, the Romans had necessarily to keep a close watch on neighbours who threatened their security. Trade was another source of information about territories beyond the frontiers. The Romans drew many of their luxuries from beyond the empire. For instance, they took supplies of amber from the shores of the Baltic. Most of their imports, however, came from the south. Ivory was obtained from equatorial Africa and frankincense from Arabia, both by way of the Red Sea. Further afield, traders took advantage of the monsoons to reach India and Ceylon in quest of spices and precious stones and it is even possible that they tapped sources as far away as South-east Asia.

A clear picture of the extent of geographical knowledge bequeathed by the classical peoples[10] is contained in the translations of Ptolemy's *Geography* which appeared in Europe during the fifteenth and sixteenth centuries. Although the maps which accompanied these had been modified to a greater or less extent to take account of new discoveries, they still show how the Mediterranean was the centre of the classical world. Yet the Romans had a good knowledge of the Atlantic shoreline from Iberia to Ireland, Britain, Denmark and the south shores of the Baltic, as well as governing some of the key provinces of temperate Europe. East of the Danube they were well aware of the nomadic peoples from the hinterland of the Black Sea to the Caspian and beyond. South of the Mediterranean their view of Africa was restricted to the north, though in the east it extended down to Ethiopia and along the east coast from the Horn of Africa to the neighbourhood of Zanzibar. Further east they occupied much of the former Persian Empire and were familiar at least with the coasts of Arabia and the Persian Gulf. Still further east they were aware of the Ganges as well as the Indus basin and Ceylon, but had only a very attenuated notion of peninsular India. Beyond that they knew of the Bay of Bengal and even had some idea of Malaysia and Indo-China. Influenced perhaps by analogy with the Mediterranean, Ptolemy was inclined to convert the Indian Ocean into a closed sea by extending the coast of East Africa to join that of south China.

Although known as the source of silk to the classical world, China remained very much on its own. The Chinese themselves had long been concerned with the extent and integrity of their own territories. References in early Chinese literature point to the existence early in the first millennium BC of a Department of Cartography responsible for housing maps that displayed the populations, raw materials and products of different regions. The earliest maps so far recovered from China date from early in the Han dynasty. These consist of silk rolls buried in a lacquer box in 168 BC with a son of the Marquis Tai, prime minister of the king of Ch'ang-sha. When unfolded, the rolls yielded two maps.[11] The larger, 96 cm square, was essentially topographical and showed rivers, mountains, settlements and roads, the latter indicated more faintly than the waterways as if to show their relative importance. The other map, which covers a smaller area at a larger scale, was concerned above all with military defences. It shows the main fortresses and the positions of encampments, road systems and waterways, as well as such details as military storage bases, watch towers and buildings suitable for military occupation. The importance attached by Chinese rulers to the extent and integrity of their realms is well documented. The founders of the first imperial dynasty, the Ch'in (221–206 BC), rose to power by defeating and annexing the previously independent principalities of the Warring States era. Their chief aim was to unify and defend their conquests. They set up a system of provinces, introduced standardized weights and measures, regularized the script used in official documents, built roads and constructed a frontier wall to defend the empire from the non-Chinese peoples to the north. The emperor in his own person was deemed to be the very symbol of Chinese unity. Under the Han dynasty (202 BC–AD 220), the empire was extended north to Korea and south to South-east Asia. There were further extensions under the Tang dynasty (618–907). In the interior, control was established over the Tarim basin and Tzungaria and diplomatic links were made with the Byzantine and Sassanian Empires. Further extensive ties were formed between ports like Canton and Yangshow and those of India and the Persian Gulf, contributing to the creation of an extensive network of cosmopolitan trade. By the time of the Ming dynasty the Chinese were playing an active role in the extension of commercial relations overseas. During the first third of the fifteenth century, that is well before Vasco da Gama had rounded the Cape of Good Hope and the arrival of Portuguese and Dutch traders in the Far East, great fleets under Cheng Ho were conducting trade with South-east Asia and south India and even taking advantage of Arabian traffic across the Indian Ocean to secure ivory from equatorial Africa.

Although geographical exploration fell very largely into abeyance on the breakup of the Roman Empire, this hardly applied to the Christian church, which during the medieval period underwent a notable northward expansion. At a time when lay authority declined, the church made the most of its opportunity. Already by the middle of the fifth century Ireland had been brought within the sphere of Christendom by St Patrick, a romanized Briton. Early medieval civilization came to Scandinavia in the form of Christianity. Norway was the first to be Christianized. Olaf Trygvason (995–1000), who had been baptized in Britain, attempted to impose Christianity on his subjects, but it was a younger member of his line, Olaf Haroldson (1115–30), a former Viking baptized in Normandy, who effectively founded the church in Norway. The Swedish king Olof Skotkonung was baptized in the year 1000. Yet it was not until around 1120 that, following a strong pagan reaction, it was found practicable to divide the country into dioceses. It was nevertheless from Sweden that Christian missionaries first entered Finland and converted the people in the course of the twelfth and thirteenth centuries. By 1293 the third Swedish crusade reached Lake Ladoga. At Novgorod it encountered an outpost of the other branch of Christendom, that of the Orthodox church based on Byzantium. Following the conversion of Vladimir, Prince of Kiev, in 988 vast tracts of Russia unknown to the classical peoples were brought within the scope of Christian influence.

The next major expansion in European consciousness took the form of direct contact with China. It is no accident that this was effected by citizens of Venice, a city which had grown rich in handling trade between the Mediterranean and the east. In 1260 the brothers Nicolo and Maffeo Polo, Venetians of Dalmatian origin, set out to trade with the Tartars beyond the Caspian. There they were persuaded to continue east and visit the court of Kublai Khan, the Mongolian founder of the Yuan dynasty of China. They were so well received that on returning to Venice in 1269 they decided to make another visit. This time they took Nicolo's son, Marco, with them. They also stayed much longer and were even pressed into the emperor's service. When they finally returned to Venice in 1295 Marco[12] wrote his *Description of the World*, a book which made an immense impression on medieval Europeans and at one stroke notably widened their apprehension of the world.

Yet beyond question it was the endeavour to reach east Asia by way of the Atlantic that was to prove decisive in opening up the world as a whole. The lead was taken by Prince Henry the Navigator (1394–1460) of Portugal, who set in motion the exploration of the coast of West Africa beyond the limits known to the Romans. By the time of his death Portuguese mariners had ventured as far as Sierra Leone. Moreover, the impetus he had given was carried forward during succeeding years and by 1488 Bartholomew Diaz had reached the Cape. At that point the king of Portugal wisely took the precaution of preparing for the next step by securing a papal bull granting him the right to acquire lands *usque ad Indos*. When Vasco da Gama rounded the

Cape he sailed half-way up the east coast of Africa before heading across the ocean to India, where he landed at Calicut in 1498 before pressing further east to establish outposts for the spice trade in the Moluccas.

Meanwhile, the Spaniards had entered the race. The marriage of Isabella of Castille to Ferdinand, heir to the throne of Aragon, in 1479, followed by the fall of the Moorish capital of Granada in 1492, made Spain the strongest state in Europe at the time. That same year Christopher Columbus made landfall on an outlier of the Bahamas, which he termed San Salvador, before going on to discover Cuba and Haiti. On his return to Spain Columbus brought back specimens of plants, birds and other animals unknown to the Old World. Although Columbus was rightly hailed as the discoverer of a New World, America took its name from his fellow-Italian, the Florentine cartographer Amerigo Vespucci. The Spaniards followed their neighbours in seeking to invoke the authority of the Pope to ensure recognition of any conquests they might make. The Treaty of Tordesillas, signed in 1494, provided that everything west of the meridian running 370 leagues west of the Cape Verde Islands off the west coast of Africa should fall to Spain, leaving Portugal with what fell to the east. Although not observed to the letter, the treaty served its main purpose, that of promoting the maximum expansion of the Catholic powers without bringing them into conflict. Many of its consequences remain. The Brazilians still speak Portuguese and the Mexicans Spanish. From Hispaniola, as they termed Cuba and Haiti, the Spaniards first ventured onto mainland America by way of Yucatán, where they made contact with the Maya Indians. They first encountered the Aztecs in 1518 and by 1520 they had effectively destroyed their empire centred on the Valley of Mexico. Ten years later they encountered the other main centre of indigenous civilization in the New World in Peru and in 1532 Pizarro overthrew the ruling Incas.

Although the Peruvians[13] were unable to oppose the Spaniards militarily because of their lack of gunpowder, they nevertheless supported a state larger than many of those found in South America today and they did so without the benefit of literacy. During the earlier phases of food production the Peruvians had existed in small local groups and it was only when more powerful cultures developed, like that of the Chimú, that wider territories linking several river valleys came into existence. The formation and maintenance of the Inca state, embracing a territory about 2,000 miles long and including a narrow coastal strip as well as the Andean highlands on which the capital city was situated, called for an altogether more elaborate system of communications. The state depended for its very existence on integrating a large and highly variegated territory.[14] The success of the Inca in maintaining their realm is all the more remarkable when we consider that their society was still preliterate, had no wheeled vehicles and depended for movement and transport on men and llamas. To offset some of these limitations the Inca could therefore make do with tracks rather than roads. Yet the nature of the terrain in the Andes was severe. The trouble taken to overcome this is a measure of the imperative need to maintain communication as the price of ensuring that the Inca realm continued to exist. In places tracks had to be stepped and zigzag up and down mountains. In others they had to be driven through tunnels or carried over swamps on stone-paved causeways provided with culverts to deal with rainfall. Narrow rivers were spanned by bridges made of stone or timber. For crossing gorges it was sometimes necessary to improvise cable bridges up to 60 m in length made from five strands of vegetable fibres, three to carry a foot-way, the others to provide hand-grips either side. The system as a whole and in particular the cable bridges needed constant repairs and attention. The local people supplied the labour necessary to keep the system in repair by way of taxes. Like the Romans, the Inca intended their system of communications primarily to serve official purposes. Resthouses were provided at four- or eight-mile intervals to give shelter to travelling officials or even the emperor himself, carried on a litter. Provision was also made in the form of shelters for the use of relays of runners to ensure the rapid transmission of official messages. By such means orders could be sent up to 150 miles a day. It was only by maintaining control over their extensive territory in this way that the Inca were able to sustain their civilization, much as, on a larger scale, the Romans had done in the Old World.

Ironically, one of the principal outcomes of gaining a foothold on mainland America was to confront the Spaniards[15] with the fact that, so far from coming upon the outposts of east Asia, Christopher Columbus had in reality found two continents which together interposed a barrier between them and their

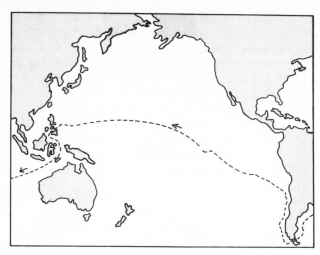

Figure 30  Map of Magellan's crossing of the Pacific, 1520–1

ultimate objective. When Vasco Nuñez de Balboa climbed a peak in Darien in 1513 he looked down on a vast ocean. The Spaniards lost no time in exploring it. As captain they chose Ferdinand Magellan,[16] a Portuguese who had gained experience in India and been present at the taking of Goa and, more to the point, of Malacca. After making an effort to find a north-west passage to the Far East, Magellan headed south. He passed down the Atlantic coast of South America and in 1520 rounded the strait that still bears his name (Figure 30). By contrast with the turbulent waters through which he had just passed, Magellan found the ocean into which he sailed, and which Balboa had been the first European to descry, relatively pacific. The new ocean, as it turned out, offered favourable currents and these carried his small fleet into the equatorial zone before making landfall in the Philippines. Magellan proceeded to annex the islands to Spain and proclaim the Christian gospel to the inhabitants, who still speak Spanish and adhere to the Roman Catholic faith. Magellan himself was unfortunate enough to lose his life suppressing a rebellion but his fleet returned to Spain by crossing the Indian Ocean and retracing Vasco da Gama's route home. When one of his ships, the *Victoria*, finally reached Spain in 1522, it had completed the first circumnavigation of the globe.

The expansion of the knowledge of the world is most accessibly documented by maps.[17] Until the sixteenth century world maps were based very largely on those transmitted by Ptolemy from the ancient world. Nevertheless, despite the capital locked up in existing plates and the high cost of making new ones, national rivalries ensured that cartographers kept in reasonably close step with the process of discovery. In his world map of 1489 Henricus Martellus, though still in general following Ptolemy, took care in delineating the coast of South Africa to take account of the voyage made by Diaz only three years previously. Giovanni Contarini showed the complete outline of Africa for the first time in his map of 1506, which also noted, even if only impressionistically, the discoveries made by Columbus. In 1529 Diego Ribeiro incorporated the outcome of Magellan's voyage although the remnants of his fleet had only completed its circumnavigation of the world seven years earlier, and Battista Agneses in his map issued from Venice in 1536 even plotted the course of the *Victoria*. Again, Blaeu's map, published in Holland in 1648 to mark the Peace of Westphalia, took account of Abel Tasman's discoveries of Tasmania and New Zealand and of his exploration of the Gulf of Carpentaria between 1642–1643 by showing outlines of a substantial part of Australasia. Such maps confirm that by the middle of the seventeenth century people were already well aware that they lived in a world very much as we know it today (Figure 31). Even so, they were still ignorant even of the coastline of parts of Australia, as well as many of the Pacific islands and the Polar regions. Again, until well into the nineteenth century knowledge of many parts of the world was confined to the coastal regions.[18] Yet by the end of the age of discovery that marked the transition to modern times cartographers were already able to provide a picture of the world as a whole, even if this was still not quite complete.

Evidence that people had begun to deal with their environment in abstract terms is to be found in the practice of adopting standard units for measuring space. How far this occurred in prehistoric times is still a matter for debate. What is certain is that it was a normal accompaniment of literate communities. The main reason for this was the need to plan more elaborate structures and undertake the more accurate planning of agricultural resources called for by more hierarchically structured

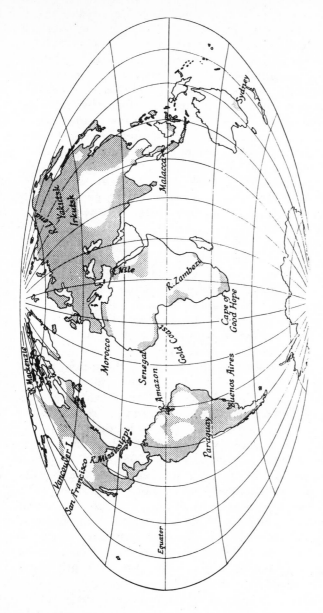

Figure 31 The world as known to Europeans c. AD 1800. Shaded areas – interior known in some detail (After Crone, *Maps and their Makers*, 1968)

societies. Until modern times units of measurement were most commonly drawn from the human body. The royal cubit of ancient Egypt, for example, was based on the length of the forearm from the elbow to the tip of the middle finger and this was subdivided into seven palms measured across the base of the fingers, or twenty-eight digits. Among other early units of space were the length of a man's foot, the breadth of his stride, and his height. Convenient as these were, they suffer from the drawback that men differ in their personal measurements. In real life people do not grow in standard sizes. Conventions had to be adopted and these differed from one community to another. While the Egyptian royal cubit was equivalent to 52.9 cm, those used by the Assyrians, for example, were 54.28 cm and by the Sumerians 49.5 cm. There is good evidence that, by using such measures, the architects and engineers of the time were able to achieve accurate results. The Great Pyramid of Egypt was constructed so precisely that though its sides were 228.6 m long they differed by less than 20.3 cm. The dimensions of the Assyrian cubit have been established by measuring the rectangular city wall of Khorsabad and taking account of inscriptions on baked clay tablets from the time of Sennacherib.

When units of measurement were formally adopted by rulers, it was customary to embody them in material form so as to be sure that adequate standards were available for checking and validating existing measures. For this purpose the ancient Egyptians made use of stone bars for recording royal cubits. The Anglo-Saxon kings of England had to put up with measures which varied in different parts of the country. As royal control increased, this was reflected in the standardization of units of measurement throughout their dominions. The first king of England to achieve this was Edward I in 1305. The iron rod on which his standard yard or ulna was marked is now lost, but the bronze bar used for the standard yard defined under Henry VIII may now be seen in the Science Museum. The standard imperial yard, legalized by statute in 1824, was ruined in the fire that destroyed the old Houses of Parliament ten years later. In 1855 it was replaced by a bar of gunmetal composed of 16 parts of copper, 2.5 parts of tin and 1 of zinc. The precise length of the standard was achieved by measuring between the intersections of finely engraved lines on gold studs set in well-holes sunk into the thickness of the bar. To ensure further accuracy the only readings accepted as correct were those taken when the temperature stood at 62°F and the barometer stood at 30 inches (76 cm) of mercury.

Although standard systems enforced in particular territories sufficed for ordinary purposes, the rise and rapid development of natural science since the closing phases of the eighteenth century have made it necessary, at least for the purposes of scientific discourse, to develop a system capable of universal application. The basic units of the metric system introduced by the French Assembly in 1799 were abstracted from the natural world by mathematics; the basic unit of spatial measurement, the metre, was defined as one ten-millionth part of the earth's quadrant passing through Paris and the litre, the basic unit of volume, as the capacity of a cubic decimetre of water.

Modern science, which began with Newtonian physics in the seventeenth century, made significant advances in several fields towards the end of the eighteenth and accelerated during the nineteenth and twentieth centuries, making a profound impact on our perception of space. For one thing it has allowed access to previously inaccessible territories, territories which, in some cases economically profitable, were in others primarily of value to scientific research. For another, and much more importantly, it has served to extend our awareness not merely of the whole range of terrestrial environments, but even more of extraterrestrial space, where space travel and the landing of men on the moon have contributed to the exploration of the limits of space and time. This has been made possible fundamentally by an increased understanding of the forces inherent in the physical world and by the development of technological skills.

The ultimate conquest of space has been achieved in effect by annihilating it as a barrier to communication. Until modern times the speed of messages, other than signals that could be transmitted by light or smoke from one point to another, was restricted to the speed at which their bearers could traverse the intervening space. It was the discovery of electricity and radio waves that first made it possible to establish contact between people widely separated in space at virtually the same moment of time. This was first achieved by telegraphy. The earliest experiments were made between 1837 and 1844, the year when Morse first transmitted dot and dash signals by cable between Washington and Baltimore. By 1851 messages were being sent by submarine cable across the English Channel and ten years later across the Atlantic Ocean. Telephony, which allowed people to communicate by speech rather than through codes, so long as they were connected by cables, first became practical as a result of Bell's patent of 1876. The first experiments in the transmission of messages without the need for wires were made by Marconi in north Italy in 1894 and in 1901 messages transmitted from Cornwall were picked up on an aerial suspended from a kite over Newfoundland, some 2,000 miles away. Shortly after the First World War programmes were transmitted on a regular basis. The process of putting people in touch, regardless of where they live, without the need to move from home, has been rounded off by television, which allows them to receive visual images. After a decade of research between 1925 and 1935 the BBC was ready to establish a regular television service. Since the Second World War television services have been provided in all parts of the world. Expansion of the coverage of individual stations has in recent years been enhanced by the ability to bounce their programmes off satellites encircling the globe. The new media have in effect reduced the world to a village and have even expanded our perception of space far beyond.

# 5

## *Civilization and the deepening of historical time*

Although history in the sense of the analytical study of documents did not appear in its modern form until the latter part of the eighteenth century, its role in chronicling the past is much older. The administration of large and complex states and the management of increasingly intricate economic, legal and religious affairs are likely to have required the use of writing and may even have been responsible for its inception. Yet it may well be that its most important role was to record the steps by which communities took shape in the course of time. In civilized states written records came to play a part comparable with that of myths and ancestral memories in preliterate ones. They endowed existing institutions with the sanction of time and in this way played a key role in maintaining the social traditions without which such states could hardly exist. By the same token the most frequent and often the only records to survive from earlier times relate to the succession of ruling authorities on whose account they were most commonly maintained.

Literacy and the maintenance of records about the past nowhere extends over more than some five millennia. It seems logical to begin with Egypt. Egypt was not only among the first countries to produce written records,[1,2] but because of the insulation of the territory and the persistence of its priestly hierarchy Egyptian records also display a most notable continuity. No attempt will be made to summarize them but the point is worth mentioning that they include structures as well as

Figure 32  The Palermo Stone, c. 2500 BC

papyrus documents. We owe our knowledge of the general scheme of Dynastic history to a compilation made around 270 BC by Manetho, a priestly chronicler, whose work has come down to us through being embodied in the writings of a later author. An example of the way earlier sources have survived is provided by the Canon of Kings, which gives a list of the rulers of Egypt up to the end of the Hyksos period towards the middle of the sixteenth century BC. This has come down to us only because some centuries later in the reign of Rameses II the other face of the papyrus was used to compile a tax-list. Among other reasons why the Turin papyrus is important is that by specifying the passage of 955 regnal years from the end of the Old Kingdom (c. 2160 BC) to the beginning of the Dynastic period it allows us to infer a date for this of around 3100 BC. Another pointer in the same direction is provided by a quite distinct source, namely the Annals carved on stone tablets at present in museums in Cairo, London and Palermo (Figure 32). Between them these records cover the reigns of the dynasties preceding the Old Kingdom, which itself began in c. 2686 BC. Although the Annals have been variously read to indicate totals of between 295 and 544 years, recent authority has focussed on a date consistent with c. 3100 BC for the beginning of Egyptian history.

It must be accepted that the priestly hierarchs were familiar with the royal succession since they were responsible for compiling the records without which they could hardly discharge their functions. How far this extended to the Egyptian people as a whole is another matter. Yet there is no need to suppose that such knowledge was restricted to the literate minority. A sense of the historical depth of their society and its rulers was displayed in a visible form by the temples founded by their kings and not least by the royal tombs and the rituals associated with them. No Egyptian could have passed his brief existence without being made aware that he lived in a community consecrated by history. The Old Kingdom pyramids were more than royal tombs by which the sons of Ra, retracing the sun's beams, ascended to heaven (Figure 33). They were the very symbols of Egyptian history, identified with kings whose place in the succession was well known. Considered merely as structures they are sufficiently remarkable. The Great Pyramid of Cheops absorbed around 2.3 million stone blocks of an average weight of more than 2,500 kg, each of which must have been floated across

Figure 33 The pyramid of Chephren, Giza, Egypt, with mortuary chapel in the foreground

the Nile from quarries on the east side and hauled overland to the point indicated by the builders. The pyramid, which covers some 5.3 ha and is some 146 m high, is almost perfectly aligned on a north–south axis and is so accurately built that the difference between the longest and shortest sides does not exceed 20.3 cm. Moreover, the stones of the outer casing are barely more than 5 mm apart. No wonder it has been acclaimed one of the most remarkable buildings ever erected! Modern architects have built structures more than twice as tall, but they have been able to do so only with the aid of modern engineering. Furthermore, no one has given a thought as to whether they will still be standing in another hundred, let alone in several thousand years. The skyscrapers of New York or Hong Kong are mere ephemeral adjuncts of a rapidly changing technological society. By contrast, the pyramids, built at an incomparably greater cost relative to contemporary means, were not designed to satisfy material needs, any more than the cathedrals of medieval Europe. They did something more. Each in their own way helped to free entire societies from the limitations that still confine non-human primates to present time.

In parts of Mesopotamia written records began to be made early in the third millennium,[3–5] but the early chronicles of this region, though comparable in age with those of ancient Egypt, are less informative to modern scholars. One reason for this is that, while the geographical circumstances of Egypt with its single river flanked by deserts favoured continuity, the twin rivers of Mesopotamia and the close proximity of highlands to the north and east created a very different environment. States were not only smaller but were subject to frequent and sometimes violent vicissitudes. Historical records were correspondingly incomplete and local. It was not until around 2000 BC that serious attempts were made to set down histories and these have only come down to us by being incorporated in later chronicles, culminating in those compiled by Berossus at the time of Alexander the Great. The fact that the king-lists for the dynasties of cities like Ur, Erech, Kish, Agade, Lagash and the rest defy attempts by modern scholars to reconstruct the early history of the country does not alter the fact that Mesopotamian scribes working in many parts of the country during ancient times found it important to chronicle successions of rulers. They would only have continued to do this if it satisfied a perceived need. When people learn to read and write, one of the first things they want to do is to record and apprehend the past, since it is the past that validates their present situation. Since the attainment of literacy stemmed from hierarchically structured societies it is not surprising that they should have directed their chronicles primarily, though by no means exclusively, to recording successions of rulers.

The prime object of early scribes was not to record precise dates. The Antediluvian king-lists of Kish assign a total of 241,200 years to eight kings and even the reigns of the twenty-three kings of the first dynasty total 24,500 years, 3 months and $3\frac{1}{2}$ days. The scribes were concerned with successions more than with the lengths of reigns. It is only with the king-lists maintained by Assyrian scribes in the eleventh century BC that we learn how their lists were in fact compiled. At that time at least, as later in classical Greece, years were designated by the names of officials. The Assyrian *limmu* lists of the time comprised the names of officials who held office for a single year.

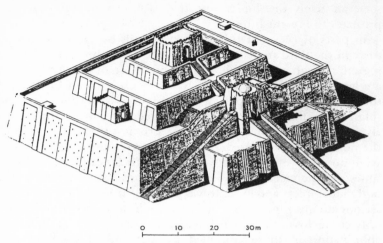

Figure 34  Reconstruction of IIIrd dynasty ziggurat at Ur, Mesopotamia, *c.* 2000 BC. (After Max Mallowan, *Early Mesopotamia and Iran*, 1965)

Kings came into it only because they customarily held the *limmu* office for a year, most often the first in their reign. Their reigns as rulers have come down to us only because the scribes commonly marked off the intervals between each king holding the *limmu* office. How far back this procedure was followed is still unknown.

An alternative way of recording the passage of historical time was to chronicle the stages in the building of major structures like the successive temples at Ur (Figure 34) or the Tummal Sanctuary in the En-lil temple complex at Nippur erected at the beginning of the dynasty of Lsin around 2100 BC. This reminds us that, as in ancient Egypt, architectural monuments of public importance evidently served to proclaim for the people the antiquity of their communities. In Mesopotamia this role was generally served by temple structures. In the case of the temple of Ninkharsag at al Ubaid, which was built in three storeys, it is particularly easy to see how social time might be measured by the progress made in the construction of buildings of outstanding symbolic status.

In view of their disturbed history it is hardly surprising that the early Mesopotamians should have concerned themselves with guidance for the future. Divination was indeed the most important discipline practised by the ancient Babylonians which they would have described as scientific. Every army had its own diviner, often a high-ranking officer, and books of omens were in sheer numbers the largest surviving category of Akkadian literature. The Akkadians most commonly made their divinations by examining the entrails and organs, notably the livers, of animals, and it may be noted that thirty-two clay models of livers were found in a room of the palace at Mari along with inscriptions dating from around 2000 BC. Among other things of which they took account was the action of oil in water and smoke from incense burning, the behaviour of animals at the gates of a city, monstrous births or portents like comets, eclipses or even downpours of rain. The Babylonians went on further, to develop astrology as a way of foretelling the future.

The Chinese[6-8] were another people to show a particularly intense concern with their history. They realized that they owed their very existence to sharing a common culture with their forebears. The fact that more than a quarter of the human race shares a common literature and cultural style is all the more remarkable in view of the varied character of their immense homeland. This ranges from the steppes bordering on Mongolia to the rain forests of South-east Asia and embraces the alluvial plains of three great rivers backed by a mountainous interior. The Chinese themselves are made up of a number of racial stocks and their spoken language varies widely in different regions. The people realize only too well that they owe their distinctive identity as Chinese to sharing a common culture. It is small wonder that this should have been permeated by a reverence for their common history and their continued adherence to a common script.

According to tradition, on the separation of heaven and earth the universe was ruled over immense periods of time by a series of god-like emperors and kings. The Han historian Sima Qian recognized the Yellow Emperor, Huang Ti, as the first human ruler, the founder-hero of Chinese civilization. The Yellow Emperor's successor founded the Hsia dynasty ostensibly around the beginning of the second millennium BC by designating his son as heir. So far the Hsia dynasty has yet to be identified for certain with archaeological data. The first dynasty to be documented by material finds is the Shang, which traditionally began in 1766 BC. The fact that the names of no fewer than twenty-

three of the thirty rulers known for this period in later compila-
tions are inscribed on oracle bones excavated at Anyang affords
strong confirmation that the Shang dynasty existed as a historical
fact. On the other hand, the first precise historical date in
Chinese history commonly accepted by scholars is 841 BC,
when a western Zhou ruler was overthrown by Kung Ho.

When the court historian Sima Qian agreed at the end of the
second century BC to compile a history of China he found
plenty of records on which to draw, left by previous generations
of court historians. So much importance was attached to history
as a guide to conduct that every effort was made to record it.
The practice was to compile the events of the previous reign on
the accession of a new ruler. In this way it was always possible to
build up a sequence of records which validated the existing
regime and reinforced the values held to be important by the
Chinese people. In assembling his material Sima Qian found it
important, like the English historian Camden, to travel widely.
In the course of doing so, it is interesting to note, he came upon
the site of the Shang capital at Anyang very much as Camden
was the first to draw attention effectively to Stonehenge.

The Chinese also displayed their concern with the past
through the study of antiquities. Apart from the large collections
accumulated in royal palaces it is known that, as early as the Six
Dynasties, between the fourth and sixth centuries AD, gentlemen
scholars had begun forming their own private ones. The fashion
reached its peak under the Q'ing dynasty when antiquarian
interests were at their height. We are only too well aware of the
kind of problem this imposes on the task of attributing ancient
artefacts to their correct period. The Chinese concern for the art
products of earlier generations resulted in a deep-seated trend
towards archaizing styles. Jade-carvers and bronze-smiths produced objects as far as possible recalling pieces several centuries
old. Instead of taking credit for originality, craftsmen aimed to
adhere to the products of earlier periods or at least to take close
account of these in shaping their own artefacts. The same applied
to painters. The four Wangs of the Qing dynasty (1644–1912),
for example, based their landscapes as far as possible on the
products of their Sung and Yuan predecessors. In the case of
porcelain it has to be accepted that the reign marks on the bases of
pots are commonly those of earlier periods. Thus, most of the
vessels with early Ming marks (1368–1644) were in fact made in

Figure 35 Terracotta figures of warriors buried in military formation at the mausoleum of the first emperor of China

the reign of the Qing emperor K'ang Hsi (1662–1722). Indeed, many pieces bearing the marks of early dynasties were really made during the nineteenth century. Jades are even more difficult to date. They show few traces of physical age and display the forms and decoration of highly traditional styles. Conscious archaizing of this kind is often and rightly criticized for encouraging virtuosity at the expense of creativity. The fact remains that Chinese art bears ample witness to the inveterate deference these people paid to their forebears.

In common with the earliest literate communities of Egypt and Mesopotamia the early Chinese marked the passage of time by the construction of outstanding monuments. A single example must suffice. Soon after becoming king of Q'in in 246 BC, Q'in Shih-hunang-ti, who became emperor of China in 221 BC, must have sanctioned the preparation of his own tomb. On his death in 210 BC he was buried, together with his childless concubines and also with those who had been engaged in the construction of his tomb. The monumental character of the tomb was visibly displayed by rectangular stone enclosures

Figure 36 Chinese oracular inscriptions on the base of a tortoise shell dating from the Shang dynasty

covering an area of some 2 square km (Figure 35). In the immediate neighbourhood of the imperial tomb four great shafts were cut, two of which contained life-sized pottery models of an army of over 1,400 warriors, including cavalry and chariots. In a third was found a military headquarters. The figures were modelled individually and finished in great detail. The emperor, in other words, was accompanied by a complete symbolic army in battle order.

That the Chinese were concerned with future as well as past time is shown by the earliest written documents recovered by Chinese archaeologists, namely the inscribed oracle bones and tortoise shells recovered from Anyang and other Shang sites

(Figure 36).[9] The inscriptions in Chinese characters were addressed to the ancestral spirits as a way of seeking guidance for future actions. The diviners sought answers to the questions inscribed by applying heat and observing the precise course taken by the cracks to which the heating gave rise. As well as helping to allay the family anxieties of leading men, notably in respect of the birth of heirs, it also enabled them to embark on journeys or undertake warlike activities with greater confidence than might otherwise have been the case.

The classical Greeks[10] showed a similar concern for the future by consulting oracles. These might be consulted at shrines in different parts of Greece, but in the course of the seventh century BC the shrine of Apollo at Delphi came to acquire a special status. On specified days enquirers who had submitted themselves to rites of purification were permitted to put questions to Apollo. The answer came through a female medium whose utterances were transcribed by the chief priest. These were often ambiguous and petitioners were thrown back on their own resources to make their interpretations. Nevertheless, the mere act of consulting the oracle was from a psychological point of view as important as any message that might emerge. At a more practical level, the Romans went to considerable trouble to ascertain from an augur whether the gods were or were not in favour of a particular course of action. Indeed, a college for training augurs was established at the very outset of Roman history. Of the five modes of divination two were regarded as of most importance, those relating to thunder and lightning and those concerned with the flight and cries of certain species of bird. In early days no act, public or private, was performed without first consulting the augurs. Even in later times, when the pretensions of the augurs were largely discounted in leading circles, the form of consultation was maintained if only to satisfy the general public.

It is commonly accepted that the ancient Greeks were much more concerned with the present than with the past. Certainly their attitude towards the past was very different from that of the Chinese or the Hebrews. Yet it could hardly be said of a people whose favourite author composed the *Iliad* that they were impervious to the appeal of the past. In transmuting folk memories of the sack of Troy passed down from the Dark Age of Greece and incorporating features derived from Mycenaean society into a work of art, Homer was feeding what must have been a deeply rooted feeling among the Greeks for their own identity. His epic satisfied the Greeks' appetite for the past without having recourse to formal chronicles. It is important to recall that the classical Greeks lacked the hierarchical social structure found in Egypt and the Middle and Far East and thus one of the principal motives for maintaining historical archives. The focus of Greek life during classical times, the polis, was a small community of free men accustomed to settling their political affairs without having to worry about the authority of leaders by validating their prescriptive rights. The individual polis kept track of its history by reference to the succession of its own officials. For a temporal sequence common to all Greeks they relied on the succession of quadrennial games traditionally held to have begun in the equivalent of 776 BC. Although at first competitors were drawn only from the Peloponnese, the Olympic Games came in time to attract competitors and spectators from all over Greece and in this way to serve as a measure of the common experience of freemen from all over Hellas.

As Bury recognized, the Greeks were by no means the first to chronicle human events. Nevertheless, they can claim to have produced the first historians and they did so primarily for political ends.[11] They pioneered looking at the past in a critical manner with a view to understanding how and why things happened as they did. They were the first to appreciate that history was worth cultivating in its own right as something to be taken into account in the conduct of present-day affairs. Although we may tend to think of Herodotus and Thucydides as Ancient Historians this is only because they wrote two and a half millennia ago. In point of fact they were modern historians in their day. Herodotus was born six years or so before the Persian War began and he lived only fifty-four years after it had come to an end. Thucydides was even closer to his subject. He was a boy of nine when the Peloponnesian War broke out and it ended five years before he died. If Herodotus is widely accepted as the father of history, this is not because he sought merely to describe the Persian onslaught on Greece. Rather it is because he considered why the conflict occurred and how the Persians failed to encompass the destruction of Greece. If he can be criticized by technical historians it is because, to the great advantage of posterity, he was unable to restrict himself to what was strictly relevant to his theme. Thucydides is rated more highly by professionals, not merely because he did restrict himself more closely to what was relevant, but because he confined himself to reliable sources and these included his own notes and speeches made when the war was still going on. Above all, he sought to account for as well as to describe the events about which he wrote.

The Romans maintained official records from early times through the College of Pontiffs, but it was only under the impact of Greek culture that they went beyond producing the material for chronicles and cultivated history. It is significant that the first Roman historian, Fabius Pictor, who wrote in the third century BC, used the Greek language. When, during the first half of the second century BC, the elder Cato wrote his *Origines* dealing with the history of Rome, he did so in Latin prose. In his choice of theme he set the course for Roman history, which was dedicated first and foremost to celebrating the foundation of the state and its expansion. It is interesting to find Livy (59 BC–AD 17) entitling his comprehensive history *Ab Urbe Condita Libri*. No doubt Livy was read widely because of his skill as a writer, but another compelling reason is that he chose a theme which went to the hearts of his fellow-countrymen. The Romans consistently used history as a means of enhancing loyalty to the state and pride in its expansion. This last became especially important during the early days of the empire. Two of the leading writers of the imperial age, Caesar in his *De Bello Gallico* and Tacitus in his *Agricola* and *Germania*, celebrated the advances of Rome north of the Alps. In their historical writing as much as in their zeal for cartography the Romans were concerned to increase support for the expansion of their empire. Again, it is significant that, in place of adopting an athletics meeting to mark their eras, the Romans preferred to use the foundation of Rome, which in terms of the Christian era is commonly set at 753 BC.

It is ironical that the Christian era began in the western part of the Roman Empire that was largely overwhelmed by the barbarians and not in the east where the empire survived for nearly another thousand years. Yet, while in Byzantium the succession of emperors continued to serve as temporal markers, in the west the collapse of the empire led to a power vacuum. Since vacuums can hardly last in respect of power any more than of time, it is not surprising that authority began to accrue to the spiritual authority already exercised by the Pope as Bishop of Rome, the ancient capital. Instead of adopting the succession of popes as temporal markers, the church accepted the birth of Christ himself as a more appropriate way of marking the course of history. The date of Christ's birth was calculated by Dionysius, an obscure monk who lived in Rome early in the sixth century and must have had access to the tables prepared by Eusebius of Caesarea (*c.* 265–339) a couple of centuries earlier. The new system was first used in Britain by the Venerable Bede in his *Ecclesiastical History of the English Nation* completed in 731. Bede took occasion to illustrate the conjunction of Christian chronology with that dating from the foundation of the city of Rome. Julius Caesar, who made his incursion into Britain in the Roman year 693, was cited as coming in the sixtieth year BC and Claudius as making his victorious entry in 798, the forty-sixth year AD.

Throughout the Middle Ages the nations that emerged from the collapse of the Roman Empire invariably sought to secure the sanction of antiquity by fostering the composition of histories. Meanwhile, the ecclesiastical authorities, who by spreading literacy made the writing of history possible and whose priests (at a time when even monarchs could rarely sign their own names) also wrote it, ensured that local sequences designated in regnal years were bound into the Christian era. Further, as apostles of a religion addressed to all men, the leaders of Christendom, lay as well as ecclesiastical, directed the expansion of European power during the age of discovery that as much as anything signalled the dawn of modern history. In the long run it was this that ensured that the Christian calendar spread worldwide. Regional affiliations like the Moslem attachment to the Prophet's migration from Medina in 622, the Hegira, or the short-lived eras of modern lay revolutionary regimes have all remained of merely local significance.

This is no occasion to embark on a review of historiography,[12] but it is worth observing that as long as the writing of history remained in the hands of the church it continued to adhere to the concept formulated by St Augustine of Hippo (354–430) in his *The City of God* that human history was ordained by God. So long as this held the field the task of the historian was primarily to chronicle how the will of God had been unfolded in the course of human affairs. Although in practice even medieval historians strayed from the narrow path, the basic idea of *The City of God* continued to influence historical thought until well into the eighteenth century. It was only in its later half that historians made serious attempts to explain the course of events in terms of reason rather than of providence. In proportion as they did so, the lead in writing history passed into the hands of philosophers like Rousseau, Montesquieu and Voltaire, or of historians such as Edward Gibbon, who sought to arrive at the truth by subjecting every available kind of evidence to critical scrutiny. The endeavour to increase the sources available to the historian contributed to the rise of archaeology during the later eighteenth century and that of technical history during the early nineteenth. In the course of his long and formidably productive life, Leopold von Ranke (1795–1886) was driven by the conviction that if he studied the documents sufficiently intensively he really could expect to discover what had actually happened in the past. If this outlook, so flattering to the technical historian, but so laughably false to the layman, still survives it only does so in societies in which, to their infinite cost, time has been deemed to be subservient to ideology. Archaeology was until very recently still conducted by the Institutes of the History of Material Culture maintained by the Soviet Union and its associates in the pious hope that, pursued with sufficient zeal, it would ultimately validate the historical philosophy developed by Karl Marx during the middle decades of the nineteenth century. Yet if history is too often pursued not to discover what happened, but to confirm what many might like to think had happened, it remains true that it is capable, if studied on its own account, of helping us to view our present situation in a temporal perspective. Whether we contemplate universal history, the history of our own society or that of any particular interest, at least it allows us to view the existing situation as the product of time. It can show us how ideas, organizations and people have undergone change as they adapted to new circumstances. Our main concern with history today must surely be with the processes which have brought about our present situation and need to be taken into account in anticipating the future.

While the Chinese, Greeks and Romans had recourse to oracles and augurs, modern Europeans have increasingly sought to probe the future by extrapolating from the past. It is only in proportion as they have succeeded in identifying the processes at

Figure 37  Egyptian shadow-clocks: (*upper*) green slate dating from *c.*
1450 BC; (*lower*) wooden, modern (From C. Singer (ed.), *A History of
Technology*, 1954)

work in history that they have been able to make intelligent
forecasts about the future. Only when existing currents have
been identified does it become possible to direct or deflect them
and so use a knowledge of the past to shape the best course for the
future. The converse is also true. The greater people's power to
determine their own direction, the more attention they need to
pay to identifying the forces that made for change in the past.
This is one reason why analytical history and archaeology
advanced at the same time and hand in hand with the natural
sciences. The better equipped people are to shape their future, the
greater the effort they are likely to make to elucidate the past and
in this way identify the basic social forces they seek to control.

A significant stage in the perception of time came when people
began to regard it as an abstract dimension rather than as part of a
cycle. A sign that they were beginning to do so came when they
began devising means for measuring its passing.[13] The commonest method used by the early civilized peoples of Egypt and the
Mediterranean world and one inherited by medieval Europe was
based on observing the orbit of the sun by measuring the shadow
cast by a gnomon or peg against some form of dial marked off in
hours. A well-known example made of green slate has survived
from the time of Tuthmosis III, who ruled Egypt between 1504
and 1450 BC, but wooden versions have continued to be used by
Egyptian peasants down to modern times (Figure 37). Sundials
fitted with gnomons to cast shadows on dials marked by
hemicircles marked off to define the hours of daylight were
widely used in the classical world and only lost their importance

Figure 38   Alabaster water-clock with outflow orifice, Thebes, Egypt, c. 1400 BC (From C. Singer (ed.), *A History of Technology*, 1954)

in medieval Europe with the invention and spread of mechanical clocks. Alternatives were instruments that measured the time taken for water or sand to pass through restricted orifices. Deep bowls with apertures to allow the escape of water were already being employed in New Kingdom Egypt and the *clepsydra* was in common use in the Mediterranean from classical times (Figure 38). Vitruvius described sand – as well as water-clocks. Hour-glasses charged with sand were especially useful in northern climates where water froze for part of the year, although at the present time they are most often encountered in the kitchen. Like sundials water-clocks remained in use well into medieval times in Europe. Indeed the market for water-clocks was strong enough in the twelfth century to support guilds of water-clock makers, who by 1220 were occupying a whole street in Cologne. Particular ingenuity was devoted to the design of water-clocks by the Byzantines. One on the east gate of the great mosque at Damascus was noted by a traveller in 1186. Brass balls were made to fall from the mouths of brazen falcons into metal cups, from which they passed through holes to a reserve. At each hour a bell was struck and another lamp was lighted high up on the gate until at dawn all went out. In this way the water-clock with its ingenious devices was made to give audible and visual warnings to the citizens of the passage of hours.

Among the first to experiment with mechanical time-keepers were the Chinese, who had been acquainted with water-clocks since antiquity. According to a text dating from 1092 they had devised an escapement mechanism to control the rotation of a wheel fitted with cups in such a way that each evacuated its water in turn at intervals of an hour. Before the Renaissance Europeans had already developed mechanical clocks, based on the movement of toothed wheels driven by weights in such a way that only one tooth was allowed to escape at a time. In respect of time-keeping the classical peoples of Europe had been no more advanced than the ancient Egyptians. It was the medieval Europeans[14] of the Gothic period who made the breakthrough in time-keeping, as shown conspicuously in architecture and maritime navigation. And they did so very largely in the service of the Christian church. It was after all Nicholas Cresinus (d. 1382), Bishop of Lisieux, who first used the metaphor comparing the universe to a vast mechanical clock created and set in motion by God so that all the wheels move in harmony. Weight-driven mechanical clocks were first developed by monks to regulate the timing of religious services. The very word 'clock' derives from the Latin *cloca*, signifying a bell. Again, the oldest surviving clock in England is that at Salisbury cathedral dating from 1386, although records show that clocks had been mounted at St Paul's, Westminster, and Canterbury during the final decade of the thirteenth century. An improved regularity in time-keeping was achieved by harnessing the cyclical motion obtained by the oscillation of a pendulum swinging under the pull of gravity. The general use of pendulums to control clocks was due to the Dutch scientist Christian Huygens during the latter half of the seventeenth century. Medieval weight-driven clocks were likely to incur daily losses of up to quarter of an hour but the use of pendulum clocks reduced this to around 10 seconds. A further improvement in accuracy was made by exploiting the flexibility of coiled springs, a development pioneered early in the sixteenth century by Peter Henlein of Nuremburg which made it possible to produce watches. Although at first these were used for jewellery, they soon came to serve as inexpensive time-pieces of the kind needed to service increasingly mechanized communities. Finally, during the twentieth century natural scientists and technologists called for degrees of accuracy beyond anything needed for daily life. One way of achieving this was to develop clocks which depended on measuring the oscillation of quartz crystals induced by alternating electric currents. Clocks of this type could be so accurate that it would take them a year or even a millennium to gain or lose a second.

As we have already observed, even prehistoric communities took thought for the future as well as the past and present in the conduct of their economies. This applied particularly to those which had adopted farming. Land had to be appropriated, cultivated and sown before crops could be harvested and stored and livestock bred, sheltered and fed to make sure that food was going to be available to the community in the future. As economies grew in complexity and scale and in particular as they had to support increasingly higher standards of living stemming from the advance of natural science, they called for the investment of capital on an ever-increasing scale. To ensure future returns investment had to be based on an increasingly sophisticated assessment of risks. The successful forecasting of future performance, whether in sport or investment, involved the discounting of risks which could only be based on the statistical assessment of past experience. Race-goers consult their form books, investors their charts, and life insurers their actuarial tables. The enhanced ability to utilize natural resources and in consequence the growth in the scale and range of capital investment has in the main been due to the development of natural science. It is hardly surprising that the rise of analytical history and archaeology should also have coincided with the emergence of natural science as a major force since the closing decades of the eighteenth century.

# 6

# Evolution and world prehistory

The question of questions for mankind – the problem which underlies all others, and is more deeply interesting than any other – is the ascertainment of the place Man occupies in nature and his relations to the universe of things.

T. H. HUXLEY

Until the rise of a more critical approach in the final decades of the eighteenth century people were happy to accept their history and the world they knew as the work of God without seeking to account for them in rational terms. The questions regarded by Huxley as of paramount importance had in fact been seriously addressed only quite recently. It is true enough that since remote times people had wondered about where they and the environment in which they lived had come from, but until modern times they were content with mythological explanations. When Sir James Frazer[1] reviewed the myths relating to the creation of the human race he reminded us that Prometheus created our first parents 'by fashioning them, like pottery, out of clay'. He went on to state that analogous myths occurred not only in the second chapter of Genesis but also in various forms among peoples as widely separated as the Pacific islanders, the Australian aborigines, the negroes of Togoland, the Eskimo of Alaska and the American Indians of California, Louisiana and Peru. It is beside the point to ask whether such myths were true. The point is that they served a purpose and met a common need, one felt as much among civilized societies as among the preliterate tribes encountered by ethnologists in the field. As the historian J. B. Bury once put it, the classical Greeks satisfied themselves with epic poetry, which for us may appear mythical but which for them could serve as history. If this could be said of the people who invented the ways of thought basic to our own civilization, we ought not to be surprised that Newton was content with Archbishop Ussher's pronouncement[2] that the world was created in 4004 BC. Newton's indifference to a question deemed by Huxley to be of the first importance reflects the fact that for a mathematician time was abstract.

Until the final decades of the eighteenth century people were largely content with classifying what they encountered in their environment and with chronicling their history. As we know from anthropology, even the simplest peoples encountered in the field had a precise knowledge of the animals and plants on which they depended. As civilized communities expanded into wider and more varied territories they experienced a need to engage in more abstract and potentially more comprehensive systems of classification. In respect of vegetation the classical Greeks had already set a good example. Already by the fourth century BC Theophrastus of Ephesus had made the primary division between monocotyledons having only one seed-leaf and dicotyledons having two that was recognized as fundamental by John Ray in his *Historia Plantarum* (1686–1704). The expansion of European exploration made it possible for Linnaeus to publish a world-wide system for classifying plants in his *Species Plantarum* published at Uppsala in 1753 as well as prompting the formation of the Royal Botanic Gardens at Kew which under Sir Joseph Banks became a main focus for classifying plants from all parts of the world. It was only when people sought to account for the diversity of species in historical terms that they found it necessary to challenge the narrow limitations on time inspired by a literal interpretation of the Old Testament.

If we are to grasp the strength of the opposition against which the pioneers of modern science had to fight in this regard, it is important to appreciate how deeply entrenched orthodox opinion was.[3,4] Protestant Christianity had from its inception been founded on acceptance of the Bible as the word of God and on a literal interpretation of its text. At a decisive period between the closing decades of the eighteenth and the middle of the nineteenth centuries this view was still widely held, not merely among people at large, but even among natural scientists themselves. The Reader in Geology at Oxford, Buckland, went on to become Dean of Westminster and it should be remembered that when Charles Darwin went up to Cambridge as a student he did so, in his father's eyes at least, with ordination as his ultimate objective.[5] Further, whatever their own views, the pioneers of modern science were acutely aware that the society in which such beliefs were widely and passionately held had the power to welcome or reject what they had to say. Acceptance of the existing order of nature, including the fixity of species, was widely held to be essential not merely to the theological but also to the social and political well-being of society at large. The decades during which geology and the biological sciences had to establish themselves were precisely those which spanned the French Revolution and the ensuing agitation for parliamentary reform in Britain. It is small wonder that one of Darwin's former mentors, the geologist Adam Sedgwick, should have regarded any move to question the intervention of divine providence in shaping the order of nature as posing a threat to the very moral and social order of civilized society as well as to Christianity itself. In the face of such an attitude it is easy to see why scientists were at pains to refer to the Creator in their writings and to leave room for his intervention even if only as the disposer of catastrophes. As we shall see, they were nowhere more circumspect than in respect of man himself.

Realization that the key to the history of the earth and of the organisms that inhabit it was to be found in the rocks which formed the terrestrial crust and in the fossils they contained first came home to scientists during the closing decades of the eighteenth century and the first half of the nineteenth. It is important to note that in his *Principles of Geology* Charles Lyell[6] defined the subject as 'the science which investigates the former changes that have taken place in the organic as well as in the inorganic kingdoms of nature'. The subject was approached from both directions. French scientists laid a special emphasis on palaeontology.[7] One of the first to appreciate the importance of extinct animals was Georges Leclerc, Comte de Buffon. Although Buffon paid a graceful compliment to the Book of Genesis by recognizing six epochs in the history of the earth, he made his own assessments of the ages of geological events:

Epoch 1 : A period of incandescence lasting 2,936 years
      2 : A period of consolidation during which hollows and ridges appeared on the earth's surface

3 : The formation of the sea through condensation over a period of between 9,000 and 12,000 years

4 : A period during which the waters sank through cracks, sea-levels fell and volcanoes became active

5 : The appearance of terrestrial animals during calmer conditions between 55,000 and 60,000 years ago

6 : The separation of the Old and New Worlds some 10,000 years ago.

The real founder of palaeontology in France, Georges Cuvier (1769–1832), recognized four distinct phases in the appearance of vertebrate animals in the fossil record: fish and reptiles, followed by Palaeotherium and Anoplotherium, mammoth and mastodon and finally man and his domestic animals. Since Cuvier still accepted that species were fixed he was constrained to attribute the succession to a series of catastrophic changes. In this he was contradicted, though not with any practical effect at the time, by Jean Baptiste Lamarck (1744–1829). Lamarck held that existing species were merely artefacts of classification. Far from being part of a fixed order of nature they were the outcome of a web of descent. Sadly for his standing among fellow-scientists Lamarck merely assumed that species transmitted characteristics acquired by reacting to changes in their environment, without suggesting whether or how this could have occurred. It was left to Charles Darwin to suggest a credible hypothesis to account for the evolution of biological species over time.

Geological stratigraphy, which afforded proof for the succession of fossils, on the other hand, owed more to German and British scientists.[8] Abraham Werner (1747–1817), whose family had been concerned with mining iron in Lusatia for three centuries and who himself taught at the School of Mines at Freiburg, laid special emphasis on the sea. He maintained that the deposition of chemical precipitates in a universal ocean held the key to the geological succession, which led to his school being termed Neptunists. In contrast, one of his former pupils, Leopold von Busch (1774–1853), who went on to hold a chair of his own at Berlin, laid greater stress on the effects of the world's internal heat giving rise to volcanic activities and in this way built up a rival school which came to be known as Vulcanists.

The most decisive breakthrough in respect of time was made by a Scot, James Hutton (1726–97).[9] In modern terms he would rank as an amateur. Certainly he was no academic. He farmed his own land, but entered fully into the intellectual life of Edinburgh at a peculiarly brilliant phase in its history. In terms of the German dichotomy Hutton was a Neptunist. He accepted that the sedimentary rocks had been deposited on the seabed, but he was also convinced that igneous ones like granite and lava must have been extruded through these in molten form from the interior. Hutton was important above all for the forthright way in which, as early as 1785, he insisted that if we would understand the history of the earth we must not expect to find the answer in human records, but in the geological deposits themselves. If we sought to understand geological history we had to do so by observing physical processes still at work in the present day. Above all we ought not to feel constrained by the traditional limits of time. How long it took deposits to form we could only hope to learn by observing processes still at work today and extrapolating from these. Hutton realized that time had better be discarded as a limiting factor in the construction of hypotheses. He concluded his *Theory of the Earth*, published in 1788, as follows: 'The result, therefore, of our present enquiry is that we find no vestige of a beginning, – and no prospect of an end.'

Although Hutton published comparatively little, his system was expounded more fully after his death by his friend John Playfair in his *Illustrations of the Huttonian Theory of the Earth* published in 1802. Above all, his basic contentions were adopted by Charles Lyell in his *Principles of Geology*, published between 1830 and 1833. Lyell insisted on the principle of uniformitarianism, that in seeking to explain geological phenomena scientists should confine themselves to processes that could be observed in action at the present day. Further, he agreed with Hutton's principle that geologists were in no way constrained by chronologies based on human records but were free to explain what they found without regard to limitations of time. It was this attitude that left Darwin free to contemplate the organic world unconstrained by traditional chronology. Indeed we know that on Henslow's advice Darwin included the first volume of Lyell's book with those he took with him on his six-year voyage on the *Beagle* (1831–6).

Darwin found Lyell's book extremely helpful in his attempts to read the geology of different parts of South America and conceived a great admiration for the author. He was greatly struck by coming upon the fossils of extinct animals like those of the giant sloths he encountered at Bahia Blanco, which needed conditions quite different from those of the present environment. On the *Beagle*'s return at the end of 1836 Darwin spent two years as one of the honorary secretaries of the Royal Geological Society in London, where he saw a good deal of Lyell, for whom he had already formed a high regard. In the course of his travels it had already occurred to him that biological species might have changed in the course of the immense periods of time opened up by the new geology. Indeed, between 1837 and 1839 he began to compile his first notebooks on the transformation of species. Meanwhile, in 1838 he chanced to read Malthus's *Essay on the Principles of Population* published forty years previously. The burden of this essay, so far as Darwin was concerned, was that many animals were equipped to expand much more rapidly than their food supply and that it was only those which succeeded in the competition for food and mates that were able to breed and contribute to later generations. This helped to concentrate Darwin's mind on what it was that made some individuals better able than others to survive. It was this that made him so preoccupied with animal and plant breeding at the time when, as a young married man, he left London to found his own family at Down in Kent. If a pigeon fancier was able to produce improved varieties by the careful selection of even slight variations, might it not be that, given time enough, nature, by selecting variants better fitted for successful competition, could have produced new species by a process of natural selection? By 1842 Darwin felt able to commit an outline of his theory to pencilled notes of 35 pages, which in the course of the next two years he enlarged to an essay of 230 pages. It was only in 1856 that Lyell prevailed on him to write at greater length, but it was not until he received a copy of an essay by A. R. Wallace from Malaya embodying basically the same hypothesis that Darwin finally consented to a summary of his own work being published alongside Wallace's essay by the Linnean Society in 1858. The following year saw the publication of *On the Origin of Species*.

Darwin himself was careful not to compromise his work by dwelling on its relevance to man. T. H. Huxley had no such compunction. As early as 1860 he launched a series of public lectures, addressed in the first instance to an audience of working men, the substance of which he published in *Evidence as to Man's*

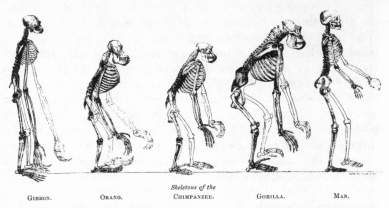

GIBBON.    ORANG.    *Skeletons of the* CHIMPANZEE.    GORILLA.    MAN.

Figure 39  Diagram of the skeletal structures of the higher primates used by Thomas Huxley as the frontispiece of his *Evidence as to Man's Place in Nature* (1863) (Apart from the gibbon, shown at twice its relative size, all are depicted at the same scale.)

*Place in Nature* (Figure 39).[10] In this he concentrated on showing how close man is to other animals by comparing their embryology as well as their general bodily structure and concluding by citing fossil skulls from Neanderthal in Germany and Engis in Belgium recovered in 1856 and 1830, which, though clearly human, nevertheless displayed primitive features that separated them from modern men. Huxley's aim, in which he largely succeeded, was to convince not merely the learned world but the general public that human beings had evolved over long periods from the Primate order, in other words that whatever their qualities they were part of the natural order. The idea of evolution had an explosive impact on people's perception of their place in time.

Transformist ideas had already begun to shape attitudes towards natural history from the closing years of the eighteenth century if not earlier, but it was not until the publication of Darwin's *Origin of Species* offered a convincing hypothesis to account for the evolution of species that their full bearing on early human history became fully apparent. If Huxley was correct, this could only be tested by anthropological research. It was necessary to recover a substantial body of hominid fossils from successive periods and subject them to the critical scrutiny of human palaeontologists. Moreover, if modern humans were in fact descended from pre-human prototypes by way of intermediate forms, it ought to be possible to trace the progressive development of the cultural behaviour that was their distinctive feature. The most direct way of doing so was to apply archaeological research to the most primitive as well as to the intervening phases of cultural history. Between them, human palaeontology and prehistoric archaeology succeeded in bridging the gap between the natural sciences and human studies and between human beings and their environments as well as extending our perception of time vastly beyond the limits of Archbishop Ussher's chronology.

Both depended on the progress of geology. The Victorians had provided ample time for the unfolding of biological change, but they remained extremely limited in respect of exact chronology until the very close of the era. In the main they had to depend on observing the thickness of successive deposits and on estimating the rate at which the deposits had accumulated. It was their lack of a precise chronology that made them so sensitive to the thermodynamic arguments for a short chronology advanced by Sir William Thompson (later Lord Kelvin), who held that the earth was losing heat at such a rate that the sun could hardly have existed for more than 500 million years, that the earth's surface would have been molten a mere 20 or 30 million years ago and that life can hardly be more than a very few million years old.

The situation was not transformed until the discovery of radioactivity in 1895. The potential of atomic decay for dating was foreseen by Rutherford in 1905, when he suggested that geological time might be measured in terms of the spontaneous atomic disintegration of radioactive materials. In the event, measurement of the rate of accumulation of helium and lead as an outcome of the disintegration of uranium became a crucial method for establishing the ages of successive geological periods. While the succession was based very largely on the organic fossils contained in sediments, it was igneous rocks that were most useful for providing radiometric dates, since adequate samples could often be obtained from lavas intercalated with the sedimentary deposits. It was by systematically applying this method between 1927 and 1959 that Arthur Holmes was able to publish absolute dates for the geological succession (Figure 40).[11,12] According to Holmes the Cambrian rocks at the base of the

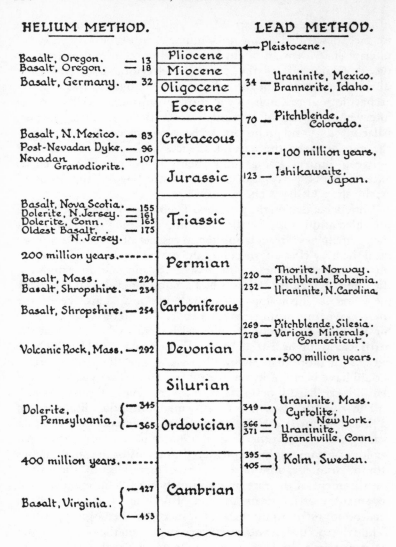

**HELIUM METHOD.**

Basalt, Oregon. = 13
Basalt, Oregon. = 18
Basalt, Germany. — 32

Basalt, N. Mexico. — 83
Post-Nevadan Dyke. — 96
Nevadan — 107
   Granodiorite.

Basalt, Nova Scotia. — 155
Dolerite, N. Jersey. = 161
Dolerite, Conn. = 165
Oldest Basalt, . — 175
   N. Jersey.

200 million years.· · · · · · ·

Basalt, Mass. — 224
Basalt, Shropshire. — 234

Basalt, Shropshire. — 254

Volcanic Rock, Mass. — 292

Dolerite, { — 345
  Pennsylvania. { — 365

400 million years.· · · · · · ·

Basalt, Virginia. { — 427
          { — 453

---

Pliocene
Miocene
Oligocene
Eocene
Cretaceous
Jurassic
Triassic
Permian
Carboniferous
Devonian
Silurian
Ordovician

Cambrian

---

**LEAD METHOD.**

←Pleistocene.

34 — Uraninite, Mexico.
    Brannerite, Idaho.

70 — Pitchblende.
        Colorado.

· · · · · · — 100 million years.

123 — Ishikawaite.
        Japan.

220 — Thorite, Norway.
    Pitchblende, Bohemia.
232 — Uraninite, N. Carolina.

269 — Pitchblende, Silesia.
278 — Various Minerals,
        Connecticut.
· · · · · · · 300 million years.

349 —} Uraninite, Mass.
       Cyrtolite,
          New York.
366 —} Uraninite,
371 —   Branchville, Conn.

395 —} Kolm, Sweden.
405 —}

Figure 40 Arthur Holmes's geological and palaeontological succession dated by radioactivity (1937)

Archaic or Primary era, which contain the first certain evidence for organic life in the form of calcareous algae and an abundant if primitive invertebrate fauna, including many genera of trilobites, brachiopods and forerunners of graptolites, began to form between 500 and 600 million years ago. The Precambrian or Archaean rocks took several times longer than the rest of the sequence combined and estimates for the age of the earth's crust ranged between 3,000 and 4,000 million years. From a human standpoint it is perhaps more relevant that vertebrates, albeit in primitive forms, first appeared at the beginning of the Tertiary between 63 and 70 million years ago and Primates during the later stages of the same era, beginning between 11 and 13 million years ago.

Some idea of the impact made by the promulgation of the doctrine of evolution is to be seen in the speed and intensity with which human palaeontology and prehistory were pursued in the immediate aftermath of Darwin's and Huxley's books. When Huxley published his *Evidence as to Man's Place in Nature* in 1863 he cited only two fossils of early man showing features more primitive than modern people, those from Engis and Neanderthal found in 1830 and 1856, though in fact a third had been found in Gibralter in 1846. By the time of the Neanderthal centenary celebrations at Dusseldorf[13] many new finds of the same kind of early man had been recovered from the Late Pleistocene deposits of Europe and the Near East. Even more significantly a different and more primitive group of early hominids had been recovered from Middle Pleistocene deposits.[14] The first, that recovered from Trinil, Java, in 1890, was treated to begin with as a kind of upstanding ape and termed *Pithecanthropus erectus* (Figure 41). Yet when comparable fossils were excavated in 1927–37 at Zhoukoudian near Peking, they were found to occur with abundant traces of cultural activity including stone tools and the use of fire. Accordingly the Peking fossils were given a special status as *Sinanthropus pekinensis*. When the focus of intensive research on human palaeontology shifted to East Africa,[15] notably to the Rift Valley of Tanzania, traces of the same kind of hominid were recovered from Middle Pleistocene deposits along with well-developed stone industries. By common consent the Middle Pleistocene hominid fossils found from East Africa to the Far East were assigned to the same species, namely *Homo erectus*. Subsequent research in East Africa

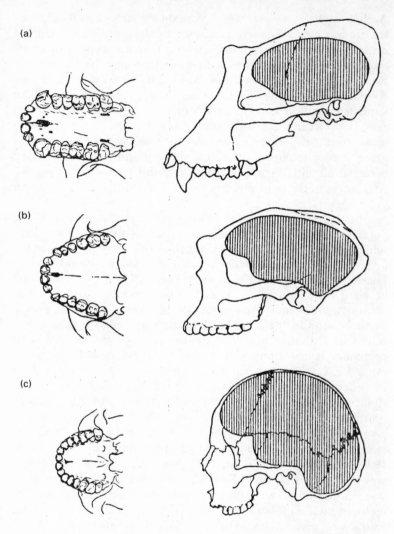

Figure 41 Diagram illustrating the reduction in dentition and the enlargement of the brain shown by comparing (a) the chimpanzee, (b) *Homo erectus* and (c) *Homo sapiens*

by the Leakey family has yielded traces of a still earlier type of tool-making man, *Homo habilis*, from deposits of Early Pleistocene age, notably from Bed I at Olduvai. One of the key questions facing human palaeontologists remains when and by what line of descent the predecessors of *Homo habilis* diverged from the Primate stem.

One group of fossil hominids to claim attention in this regard is the australopithecines originally identified in South Africa but latterly recovered by the Leakeys in East Africa. These owe their main interest to students of hominid evolution to their upright stance. This could already be inferred from their skeletal remains but has since been confirmed by the discovery at Laetoli in northern Tanzania of the footprints of two or three individuals impressed on a tuff surface (Figure 42). The importance of an upright stance is, of course, that it frees the forelimbs from the task of locomotion and makes them available to explore and manipulate the immediate environment. The fact remains that it is generally agreed that the more robust *Australopithecus robvstus* became extinct without contributing to human evolution and though some have argued that the more gracile *A. Africanus* did, many regard it as a cousin rather than a direct ancestor of *Homo*.

Our first undoubted ancestor, *Homo habilis*, appeared in Bed I at Olduvai and, according to potassium argon analysis of the volcanic sediments in which the remains were found, dates from around 1.7 million years ago. When modern humans first appeared is still very much a matter for research. Recent work by molecular biologists[16] on mitochondrial DNA points to their emergence in Africa between 150,000 and 200,000 years ago. On the other hand, the first decisive evidence stems from their expansion late in the Pleistocene over temperate Europe and adjacent parts of south-west Asia, alongside material evidence for cultural innovation on a broad front. It is becoming increasingly evident that a close and probably reciprocal relationship existed between the biological and cultural advance of modern humans. Indeed, there are strong grounds for regarding them as artefacts of their own culture. At the very least there was a strong interaction between cultural and biological development. Until the Late Pleistocene their culture remained rudimentary and more or less uniform. It is significant that the last 50,000 years have witnessed a marked acceleration in both their biological and their cultural development, including a notable increase in

Figure 42  Laetoli: footprints of *Australopithecus*

the diversity of their artefacts. Even in the aberrant Neanderthal form *Homo sapiens* expanded far north over much of the Soviet Union and may have already begun to accord burial to his dead. Yet it is only in the modern form of *Homo sapiens sapiens*, to which all the existing human races belong, that we have evidence of a distinctively human range of cognition. As Gordon Childe implied in the title of his popular book *Man Makes Himself* men have only experienced their full humanity to the extent that they have modified their behaviour in accordance with culture.

In summary, geology and human palaeontology both suggest that, biologically speaking, human beings had no sudden beginning. Our forebears emerged from the other Primates in the course of evolution and the Primates themselves first appeared during the late Tertiary period that began between 11 and 13 million years ago. If we accept potassium-argon dating, the first humans had appeared by 1.7 million years ago. The precise antecedents of modern humans remain to be determined, but anthropologists now accept that anatomically modern people existed around 100,000 years ago. To judge from the evidence of prehistoric archaeology it would seem that a cultural threshold was passed some 30,000 years ago, marked by the appearance of a variety of specialized tools and weapons, personal ornaments and symbolic art in the present temperate zone, most notably in Europe. The first literate communities did not appear until some 5,000 years ago and then only in narrowly defined areas of north-east Africa and south-west Asia.

Archaeology has been studied in Europe since the sixteenth century. To begin with it took the form of antiquarian studies devoted to amplifying the earliest written records. The notion that knowledge of the past could be extended beyond the range of written records by studying the detritus of human societies first took shape effectively during the late eighteenth and early nineteenth centuries.[17] By the 1820s antiquities from the prehistoric period had accumulated to the point at which it became increasingly necessary to classify them. This was especially true of northern Europe. In 1836 C. J. Thomsen of the National Museum at Copenhagen published the scheme he had used for some years to display the collections under his charge. Thomsen's Three Period System proved so useful that his book was widely translated and helped to lay the foundations for a systematic study of prehistoric archaeology. Yet the point needs to be made that the prehistory envisaged by Thomsen could have been readily accommodated within the confines of Archbishop Ussher's biblical chronology.

It is significant that discoveries which did not fit in with this were either ignored, rejected or explained away until the idea of evolution had been promulgated by Darwin. When Dean Buckland, Reader of Geology at Oxford, came across an ochre-stained skeleton in the cave of Paviland, he blithely assigned it to the Romano-British period, even though it occurred alongside the skull of an elephant. Again, when Boucher de Perthes, the French customs official, described the flint hand-axes he had found with remains of extinct animals in the gravels of the Somme at Abbeville, his book was generally ignored until in 1858–9 his finds had been inspected by a succession of British geologists and archaeologists, including Falconer, Lyell, Prestwich, John Evans and Sir John Lubbock. One of Evans's first tasks on his return to London was to re-examine the flint hand-axes recovered by John Frere in 1787 under 12 feet (3.5 m) of brickearth at Hoxne in Suffolk and deposited in the keeping of the Society of Antiquaries of London. In communicating his original discovery to the Society generations previously, Frere had expressed the opinion that they must belong to a very remote period. It was only in the wake of Darwin and Huxley that their true significance was recognized.

The excitement generated by the idea of evolution found expression in other ways, notably in a spate of lectures and publications ranging over the entire field of anthropology. One of the most active figures was Sir John Lubbock, whose *Prehistoric Times,*[18] published in 1865, incorporated the substance of lectures given during the previous four years and printed in a variety of British, French and American journals. Lubbock's book is famous in the history of archaeology as being the first to divide the Stone Age into a Palaeolithic phase, during which men existed alongside extinct animals and lived exclusively by hunting, fishing and gathering, and a Neolithic one marked by advances in the working of flint and stone, by pottery-making and weaving and not least by the practice of farming. His book is also important for the insight it gives into the concepts that stemmed from the idea of evolution. For one thing Lubbock discussed prehistory in purely naturalistic terms. In addressing the antiquity of man he drew on the evidence of geology,

palaeontology and even astronomy. He discussed human biological and cultural evolution in universal terms. He felt as free as
any scientist to draw upon data from whatever period or part of
the world it came. In the case of archaeological data, although his
own direct experience was limited to Europe, he had no
compunction in drawing upon evidence from India or the New
World. Yet although Lubbock and his generation were liberated
by the idea of evolution, they were in some danger of being
enslaved by it. He and his contemporaries failed to recognize that
human societies, by the mere fact of their being human and
subject to history, needed to be treated differently from animal
species. In devoting three of his sixteen chapters to the 'modern
savages' who at the time of their discovery were ignorant of
metals, he did so in the simple expectation that they might be
able to throw direct light on the remains of savage life in ages
long past. Even some modern writers have failed to take account
of the degree of diversity displayed by the peoples of southern
Africa and Asia, Australia and Oceania, not to mention those of
the New World, from the Eskimo in the far north to the
Patagonians and Fuegians in the extreme south.

    The drive to trace the evolution of human culture and so
bring about a deeper historical awareness involved the laborious
recovery of archaeological data from stratified deposits. This
began in western Europe, where the idea of evolution had first
been developed. So far as the Palaeolithic Stone Age is concerned, the lead was taken by French prehistorians, who were
exceptionally well endowed with stratified caves and rock-
shelters as well as with river terraces rich in fossils of the earliest
phases of European culture. When the earliest textbooks began
to appear soon after the First World War they were largely based
on the Palaeolithic sequence established in France by G. de
Mortillet in 1881 and revised by the Abbé Breuil in 1912.
Inevitably the French sequence tended at first to be applied to
discoveries made in other parts of Europe. It was only when
excavators began to study material from central and eastern
Europe, North Africa and south-west Asia that they came to see
that the French sequence enshrined in textbooks was in fact of
only local application. As archaeologists the world over busied
themselves with establishing local sequences, it became increasingly important to synchronize those recognized in different
parts of the world. Regional sequences could be linked to

geological changes, but their correlation could only be effected at the cost of time-consuming and costly research.

That is why radiocarbon dating,[19] a method capable of being applied the world over, received such a warm welcome from prehistorians. It all began when Willard Libby decided to test whether radiocarbon (C-14), generated at high altitudes through the interaction of cosmic ray neutrons and atmospheric nitrogen, was present in living matter. Radiocarbon enters into the carbon dioxide of the atmosphere and is taken in by green plants through photosynthesis. It thus enters the food chain, becoming part of all living creatures. When Libby and his team at the Institute of Nuclear Physics at Chicago undertook tests in 1947 they found that methane from Baltimore sewage contained radiocarbon in the predicted amounts, but methane from petrol, being far more ancient, produced hardly any. This was consistent with the tenet that, whereas in life organic material absorbs radiocarbon at the same rate as it loses it by decay, it ceases to do so at death. From this point the radiocarbon content decreases because of radioactive decay. Since the half-life of C-14, that is the time it takes to lose half its radioactivity, has been determined (approximately 5,568 years), it follows that measurement of the residual radiocarbon radioactivity in an organic sample should allow an estimate of its age to be made. The precision of this estimate is limited by the nature of the disintegration process, and the uncertainty of the age is governed by the standard deviation of the measured sample radiocarbon activity. This means that the pattern of radiocarbon ages of samples, especially when there is stratigraphic control, is of greater significance than a single determination. Since the older the sample the smaller the residual activity and the greater the statistical uncertainty, radiocarbon chronology can only usefully be applied to samples dating from the last 50,000 years or so, a period which nevertheless encompasses the main achievements of modern humans. It is also important to note that, owing to long-term variations in the atmospheric radiocarbon content, radiocarbon years are not consistently equal to solar years. The overriding fact remains that the disintegration of carbon proceeds at the same pace the world over. Libby and his colleagues recognized the significance of this crucial fact in their first book, which included determinations of historically dated samples from Egypt, along with prehistoric ones from Europe and south-

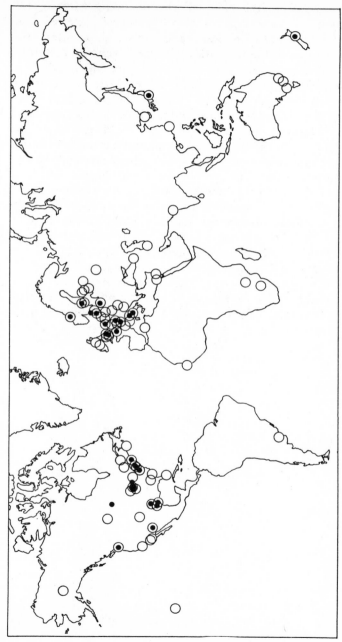

Figure 43  Map showing the worldwide spread of radiocarbon dating laboratories:
● The original station at the Institute of Nuclear Studies, Chicago
● Stations operating at the time of the first issue of *Radiocarbon* (1955)
○ Stations operating in 1977

west Asia and from the New World, including Mexico and South America as well as the United States itself. One result of the method's being of world application is that laboratories were rapidly set up in all the scientifically more advancecd countries of the world (Figure 43).[20] One of the topics on which radiocarbon dating has thrown crucial light has been the expansion of human settlement over northern Eurasia to Japan, the colonization of Australasia and the Pacific and not least the occupation of the New World from northern Canada to Patagonia in the extreme south.[21] Another has been the light it has thrown on the adoption of more productive methods of subsistence and the rise of civilizations in different parts of the world. Perhaps the best idea of the impact of the new method of dating provided by physics is given by Australia. Without his chronological archive formed by radiocarbon determinations it would have been quite impossible for John Mulvaney to have written his *Prehistory of Australia*.[22] When the white man arrived in 1788 the aboriginal inhabitants were still prehistoric. They could only perceive their own past through myths, rituals and ancestral memories. In our own generation we have been able to visualize our past as human beings in the context of geological time and the prehistoric basis of our recorded history.

# 7

## *Extraterrestrial space and time*

The totality of space is the universe, and the totality of time is the history of the universe.

P. C. W. DAVIES

From early times people have been aware, even though they may have had limited perceptions of space and time on earth, that they had only to look to the heavens to see that their world was not alone in the universe. As we have seen earlier, even preliterate peoples observed the heavenly bodies and took careful note of their movements within the limits of what they could observe by the naked eye. They did so wherever they were and however they earned their living. On land they sought guidance in scheduling the food-quest, whether this was based on hunting and gathering or on different kinds of farming. Success depended on timing and this was most effectively achieved by keeping a close watch on the sun, moon, planets and visible stars. Economic factors were by no means the only ones involved. Magic, the notion that human fate was ultimately controlled by conjunctions of the heavenly bodies, also played its part. When the ancient Babylonians scrutinized the heavens, they did so not so much to satisfy their intellectual curiosity or in any spirit of abstract meditation, so much as to consult what they regarded as the masters and rulers of the world and the governors of human life. In a word they viewed the heavens not as astronomers, but as astrologers.

The first to engage in scientific astronomy,[1] that is in the precise and systematic study of the heavenly bodies and their movements as an end in itself, were the geometers and mathematicians of classical Greece. In the sixth century BC Pythagoras was already teaching that the world was spherical, that it rested without support at the centre of the universe, that each of the planets orbited the sun attached to revolving crystal spheres and that beyond them the fixed stars were attached to an outermost one. The Greeks even went some way to establishing the dimensions of the heavenly bodies and the distances between them. During the fourth century BC Aristotle concluded that the moon was closest to the earth and early in the third Aristarchus of Samos calculated that the sun was twenty times more distant from the earth than the moon. He also estimated that the diameter of the moon was only a third that of the earth. As for the earth itself Eratosthenes (276–196 BC) calculated that its circumference was around fifty times the distance between Alexandria and Syene. Further progress was made by the inventor of trigonometry, Hipparchus (190–120 BC), who held that the moon was about fifty-nine times as distant from the earth as the earth's radius. This implied that the average distance of the moon from the earth would have been around 24,000 miles, which differs by less than a thousand miles from the modern value reached by measuring the time taken by an electromagnetic current to reach the surface of the moon and return to earth. The ancient Greeks were much less successful in estimating the distance of the earth from the sun. By modern standards, that proposed by Aristarchus of 4,800,000 miles was about twenty times too small. What is nevertheless clear is that Greek thinkers were already contemplating distances far exceeding anything on earth.

Knowledge of ancient Greek astronomy has come down to us in the main through the compilation made by Ptolemy (AD 90–168) at Alexandria. The *Almagest*, as it was termed by the Arabs, first became accessible to Europeans when the Arabic text was translated under the emperor Frederick II around 1230. In the absence of further original research Ptolemy's *Almagest* held the field until the end of medieval times in Europe. Indeed it was the supersession of the Ptolemaic system that, along with the discoveries made by navigators during the age of discovery, formed the main watershed between the medieval and modern phases of European history. The first to question the Ptolemaic picture of the heavens was the Polish priest Copernicus (1473–1543). During the last thirty years of his life Copernicus suggested that, so far from being a fixed point at the centre of the universe, the earth rotated on its own axis and revolved around the sun. Further, he held that the distant stars beyond the sun and its planets, from the mere fact of their appearing to be fixed, must be infinitely remote in space. In effect, by proposing a heliocentric in place of a geocentric system and hinting at a great enlargement of the universe, Copernicus was inviting a revolutionary change in people's perception of the world and of its place in the universe, just as the expansion of geographical knowledge had made it redundant to place Jerusalem at the centre of the world. As C. S. Lewis once observed, the close of the Middle Ages was marked above all by the discarding of Christendom as the focus of the world and of the world itself as the centre of the universe.

The Copernican system was not at first widely accepted. For instance the famous Danish astronomer Tycho Brahe (1546–1601), while ready to allow that the other planets orbited the sun, continued to hold that the sun as well as the moon orbited the earth. The first leading astronomer to adopt the heliocentric system fully was the Italian Galileo (1564–1642), whose interest in mechanical devices led him to adopt at the earliest opportunity the telescope invented by Hans Lippersheim and presented to the General States of Holland in 1608. Since prehistoric times knowledge of the heavens had been limited to what could be seen by the naked eye, aided by such instruments as the astrolabe described by Ptolemy and available to Tycho Brahe. By using a simple telescope comprising a tube holding a convex lens designed to produce at its focus an image of a distant object and provided with a magnifying glass as an eyepiece, Galileo was able to observe four moons orbiting Jupiter. It was this that convinced him that the traditional geocentric view could hardly be correct. On the contrary, he became certain that Copernicus, despite having been largely ignored, was in fact right. Galileo was a man of sufficient weight to constitute a threat to the orthodoxy held by the church that he could hardly avoid its condemnation. Although he found it politic at first to accept the injunction to desist from teaching the heliocentric system, he was unable to resist publishing an imaginary dialogue between its advocates and opponents. This so much alarmed the authorities that they were stung into taking drastic action. Galileo was seized by the Inquisition, imprisoned and made to abjure his teaching under oath. In fact he was being made to pay for an idea formulated by a man who had already died nearly nine decades previously. The reaction was too late. The Inquisition had precisely no effect on people's perception of the universe, unless it was to endow Galileo with the prestige of martyrdom and for the first time focus attention on the Copernican view of the solar system. The time was now ripe for a profound enlargement in the understanding of the universe.

In developing the ideas which were basic to modern physical science, Isaac Newton repeated some of Galileo's experiments. Like him, he rolled balls of different weights down a smooth slope to measure their speeds because he realized that it would be easier to calculate their velocity in this way than if they had been dropped from a height. Newton's first law of motion was in fact that bodies increased in speed regardless of their weight and his second that a body would accelerate in proportion to the force applied to it. Newton's importance as a physicist is that his laws concerning matter applied throughout nature from the smallest particles to the entire universe. Further, he not only advanced a theory to account for how bodies moved in space and time, but developed the mathematics needed to analyse their motions. His theory of gravity, that bodies are attracted to one another with a force proportional to their mass and inversely proportional to the square of the distance between them, applied throughout the universe. He appreciated that, since according to his theory the heavenly bodies must attract one another, they can hardly have remained motionless. Indeed, his great achievement was to account for their movements. For Newton one of the main tasks of the physicist was to explain how it was that the universe in fact operated in a predictable manner. It was a prime task of physics to forecast the motions of the sun, moon and planets to a high degree of accuracy. The Royal Observatory was founded at Greenwich in 1675 with the very practical object of determining longitude at sea. That is why Edmund Halley, who later became Astronomer Royal, entered so keenly into discussions with Newton and not only urged forward but actually paid for the publication of the *Principia* in 1687. Halley himself was to owe his popular fame to his successful prediction of the return in 1758 of the comet whose appearance in 1066 had been featured on the Bayeux tapestry and which had most recently appeared in 1531, 1607 and 1682. Newton's work provided a theoretical basis for a fundamental advance in human understanding of the behaviour of the heavenly bodies.

The nearer planets – Mercury, Venus, Mars, Jupiter and Saturn – had already been observed by the ancients, but those more distant from the sun were only brought within human cognizance with advances in the design of telescopes during recent centuries.[2] Uranus first took its place in the solar system in 1781 as a reward for Herschel's efforts to improve telescopes and so widen the range of astronomical observation. When Uranus came under close scrutiny it was found to display perturbations which led astronomers to infer that some other body must be exerting a gravitational pull. After French and British mathematicians had computed its likely position astronomers sought to identify it by observation. This was achieved in 1846 when the planet Neptune was picked out by the telescope. Even so, some traces of perturbation remained and the search was on to identify a further planet. This was accomplished at the Flagstaff Observatory, Arizona, in 1930, when the discovery of Pluto completed the solar system. So far as size was concerned the classical Greeks had made a reasonably close estimate of the distance of the moon from the earth, but had fallen miserably short when it came to the distance of the earth from the sun. Modern astronomers equipped with telescopes have determined the distances of the planets from the sun in terms of millions of miles as follows:

| Mercury | 36 |
| Venus | 67 |
| Earth | 93 |
| Mars | 141.5 |
| Jupiter | 483 |
| Saturn | 886 |
| Uranus | 1,783 |
| Neptune | 2,793 |
| Pluto | 3,666 |

Although these distances may seem large by comparison with those on earth, they are small indeed by comparison with the universe at large. One way of bringing this home is to express them in terms of the speed of light. The notion of expressing distance in terms of time is familiar in daily life. We know very well what it means to speak of a day's march or of a voyage of so many days, weeks or months. Because of the enormously greater distances with which they have to deal, astronomers are accustomed to using the speed of light, the medium through which, after all, information about outer space reaches us, as a unit of measurement. Taking the speed of light as equivalent to covering 186,000 miles a second we obtain a useful unit of travel time. In this way we can speak of the maximum distance on earth as the equivalent of 1/20th of a light-second or of the sun being some 8 light-minutes distant from the earth. Another way of looking at it would be to say that we can see the sun as it was 8 minutes ago. In terms of light travel even the most distant planet, Pluto, is only some 5.5 light-hours distant from the sun and the solar system itself a bare 10 or 11 light-hours across by comparison with the millions of light-years accommodated in the universe.

After establishing the composition and scale of the solar system, it remained to examine more closely its constituent parts and then go on to establishing its context in the universe. The first is still being accomplished by despatching spacecraft to approach or even land on the surface of our moon and the other planets in the solar system. The basic appeal of Jules Verne's fiction is that, while opening up exciting prospects, it did not go too far ahead of existing experience. A hot air balloon had already carried two men over Paris some eighty years before he published *Cinq semaines en ballon* and the concept of propelling men to the moon embodied in *From the Earth to the Moon* appealed to a public ready to overlook the lethal effect of being fired from a giant cannon. The artificial satellites used today to gather information about the solar system are safely thrust into orbit by means of rockets, the prototypes of which were invented by the Chinese and used in warfare by medieval Europeans before being displaced by artillery. The rockets used in modern space research stem directly from those trained on Britain by the Nazis during the Second World War. In adapting these to launch satellites it was necessary to use more effective fuels and produce stepped rockets designed to fire in successive stages so as to carry well clear of the earth's gravitational field.

The Americans took the lead in announcing their intentions, but it was the Russians who in 1957 were the first to put an artificial satellite into orbit. Although Sputnik was less than 2 feet (0.6 m) in diameter, it carried a wireless transmitter which alerted the world to the fact that the race in space had begun. In 1958 the Americans responded by launching their first satellite, but the Russians resumed their lead by landing a series of probes

Figure 44 The American cosmonaut Buzz Aldrin fixing seismic equipment on the surface of the moon

on the moon. Significantly, the third of these, Lunik III,
succeeded in transmitting photographs of the moon's far side.
Even more notably the Russians succeeded in launching a
human astronaut, Yuri Gagarin, in Vostok I and in returning
him safely to earth. The Americans replied by putting their own
astronaut, John Glenn, into orbit and retrieving him. In 1966 soft
landings were made on the moon and photographs of the lunar

surface transmitted back to earth. The climax came when, a little more than a century after Jules Verne's fiction, the Americans landed Neil Armstrong and Edwin Aldrin on the surface of the moon and listeners heard Armstrong's actual words as he set foot on it (Figure 44). As if to bring home the reality of making lunar territory accessible, the Americans next proceeded to land a wheeled vehicle and drive it briefly over the surface of the moon.

The prodigious cost of maintaining space research would only have been incurred in anticipation of substantial returns and it seems important to consider what these were. The military advantages hardly need stressing, more particularly in respect of Intelligence. The economic potential is equally evident. As recently as 1988 the National Research Council managed to thwart or at least to delay the setting up of a Commercially Developed Space Facility to oversee the manufacture in a micro-gravity environment of such substances as ultra-pure pharma-ceuticals and perfectly formed crystals. The mere fact that such a step was even proposed serves to emphasize the economic potential of space research. Yet its chief prize is the prestige of heading the race to advance natural science. It is for this above all things that the superpowers competed, very much as the nation-states of western Europe competed to advance navigation in the age of exploration that marked the onset of their modern history. The Soviet Union has given impressive evidence of this in its steadfast determination to establish a permanently manned satellite orbiting the earth. On this scientists would be able to conduct long-term experiments working beyond the earth's atmosphere, reinforced by relays shuttling to and from ground bases. In the long term space research, like other fields of scientific endeavour, resulted in making human beings freer of their immediate environment, more able to shape it to their will and more fully aware of their own context in time and space.

If the exploration of the solar system has greatly extended our perception of space, the study of the universe as a whole has also made us aware of hitherto unimaginable vistas of time. The existence of outer space far beyond the sun and planets has long been evident to anyone who scrutinized the night sky even directly through his eyes. As a way of mapping what appeared to be patterns of stars observers from at least the third millennium BC in Mesopotamia had found it useful to designate particular groups and name them after familiar animals and artefacts or

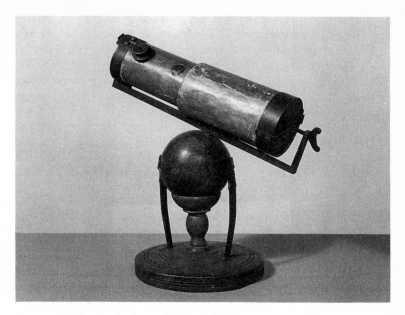

Figure 45  Newton's first reflector telescope

even mythical human beings. According to Ptolemy's *Almagest* the northern hemisphere displayed some forty-nine named constellations. From early times the Milky Way had also attracted attention as a luminous wavy band across the heavens. It was only when Galileo turned his newly acquired telescope upon this that he saw it to be composed in reality of a multitude of distant stars. From the mere fact that they did not appear to be affected by the gravitational pull of the sun Isaac Newton argued that they must be extremely remote.

Newton by no means confined himself to theory. On the contrary, he engaged actively in observing the movements of the heavenly bodies and helped to inaugurate the programme of exploration continued in recent centuries (Figure 45). To assist him he constructed a telescope with a reflector in place of the lenses used in the old refractor telescopes, to avoid the false colours produced by the glass lenses of earlier models. Further notable advances were made by William Herschel (1738–1822), who used reflector telescopes of his own manufacture. Although most widely known for his discovery of Uranus and its two satellites, Herschel made his greatest contribution in many respects by his examination of the Milky Way, which he saw as a disc-shaped aggregation of stars, incorporating the sun. He also made important contributions through his study of nebulae. Where Halley had known of six and the French astronomer Messier listed over a hundred in 1781, Herschel added over another 1,500. Furthermore, he suggested that some of these might well be separate galaxies far beyond the limits of the Milky Way. In this he had in fact been anticipated by the philosopher Immanuel Kant. In his *Theory of the Heavens* published in 1755 the philosopher had elaborated the idea set out by the mathematician Thomas Wright of Durham five years earlier that in reality there were numerous Milky Ways. The philosopher Kant went further and painted a picture of the galaxies beyond the Milky Way being grouped in clusters which in turn formed larger systems. At the ultimate level of infinity Kant believed there must be an ultimate cosmic centre.

As conceived by Newton the universe resembled a clockwork which conformed in its motions to the laws of gravity. Accordingly the prime function of astronomy was to observe and verify the movements of the heavenly bodies. This involved the invention and use of increasingly more effective apparatus. No attempt will be made here to trace the history of this in any detail. The point to emphasize is that improvements in astronomical instruments reflect man's anxiety to enlarge his perception of space as much as his keenness to improve navigation at sea. Ironically also it was the increased depth of understanding of the universe beyond the limits perceived by Newton that finally exposed the limitations of his system and paved the way for a more dynamic cosmology.

The most important improvements lay in the size and quality of the lenses or reflectors used. The invention of achromatic glass lenses during the latter part of the eighteenth century answered Newton's main complaint and encouraged a return to refracting telescopes. On the other hand, because the limit for glass lenses was 40 inches, when larger telescopes came into use in modern times these were of the reflector type. The increasing size of telescopes brought its own problems. The greater the magnification the more restricted the zone visible at any one time and the more important it became to ensure smooth and rapid shifts in direction. Similarly, the larger the reflector, the weightier the mounting. Astronomers had increasingly to rely on massive power-driven telescopes. The application of photography to astronomy around the middle of the nineteenth century was another factor of great importance. Images recorded on film are more dependable than those observed by the human eye. The camera is tireless, makes no mistakes and produces permanent records capable of direct comparison with earlier ones. Not surprisingly the discoveries made by modern visual astronomy depended at first almost entirely on images recorded by the camera.

Outstanding advances in astronomical knowledge were made as the giant American telescopes came into play (Figure 46). When Edwin Hubble deployed the 100-inch reflector telescope at Mount Wilson, California, in 1917, he immediately doubled the depth to which astronomers were able to see into the universe. In opening up a zone some 500 million light-years in depth he enlarged the numbers of known galaxies from half a million to around 100 million. To form some idea of what this involved we have only to reflect that our own galaxy, the Milky Way, comprises some 4 billion stars including our own sun. If Hubble did so much to extend our comprehension of space he did even more to deepen our conception of time. Above all, his discovery in 1929 that the universe is in process of expansion meant that it could no longer be regarded as a machine, but rather as part of an evolutionary process. In other words he brought cosmology, hitherto a preserve of traditional mythology, into the sphere of physical enquiry just as Hutton had done in respect of the earth and Darwin in that of living organisms.

Once the origin of the universe had been brought within the compass of natural science, it followed that such an absorbing topic attracted wide interest not only among scientists[3-7] but also among a wider public. The first model to gain widespread acceptance was the steady state theory formulated by Hermann Bondi, Thomas Gold and Fred Hoyle in 1948. According to this, the universe was deemed to have no beginning or end. As galaxies moved away from each other new ones continually filled the gaps. The steady state theory had no sooner gained wide acceptance than it was overtaken by the results obtained by another Cambridge group, this time led by Martin Ryle, by means of radio astronomy,[8] between the late 1950s and the early

Figure 46 Edwin Hubble with 40-inch Schmidt telescope at a time when the recession of the galaxies was accurately measured

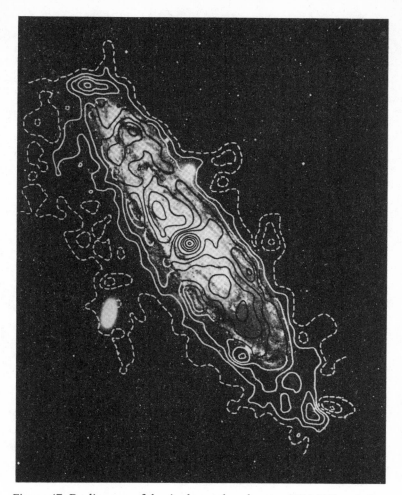

Figure 47  Radio map of the Andromeda galaxy at 408 MH2 superim-
posed on an optical picture (From D. W. Sciama, *Modern Cosmology*,
1971)

1960s (Figure 47). Radar had been invented only in 1939, just in
time to locate enemy aircraft and direct anti-aircraft batteries
during the Second World War. After the war was over astronomers were able to lay their hands on surplus equipment and
expertise and radar was applied to astronomy by Bernard Lovell
at Jodrell Bank and at Cambridge by Martin Ryle. Unlike the

steady state theorists, Ryle and his team held that the universe had begun at a moment of time.

According to the big bang theory, as it came to be known, all the galaxies in the universe must originally have been squeezed into a single mathematical point of infinite density. Before the big bang some 10 billion years ago, nothing could have happened because there would not only have been no matter, but no space and no time. The big bang would in some ways have been even more profound than the biblical creation because this posited a pre-existing void. Unlike the proponents of the steady state theory, Ryle and his followers concluded that the universe had begun and might by implication be expected to end at a moment of time. According to the big bang hypothesis, the beginning of the universe could be traced back to the first second of its existence. It was only this that remained beyond the range of physics. In the beginning the universe would have been not only highly compressed but also extremely hot, forming a veritable fireball with temperatures of the order of 1,000 billion degrees. It was only as temperatures moved down to a few billion in the course of the first few seconds that neutrons and protons began to combine to form nuclei. Only then could organized structures become possible and the universe as we know it, with its hierarchy of stars and planets grouped in galaxies, themselves bunched in clusters, come into being as the outcome of an evolutionary process. Modern cosmologists have not by any means been the first to appreciate that the universe has been and remains a theatre of violent change. Early peoples not only observed the appearance of comets but also noted other signs that the heavens reflect more than cyclical changes. For instance in 1054 the Chinese observed that the Crab nebula glowed a hundred times brighter after having undergone several months of fading. Among the many triumphs of radio astronomy was the discovery in 1967 of pulsars generally interpreted as the remnants of the deaths of stars. It is now thought that the sun, a star of average mass, was formed only about 5 billion years ago and that the earth and other planets of the solar system stemmed from a disc formed around it. The big bang theory received considerable support in 1965 from the discovery by Penzias and Wilson of micro background radiation which apparently reaches us from across most of observable space and which they interpreted as reflecting the glow of the early universe.

Although Stephen Hawking[7] has recently expressed himself as being 'fairly confident that we have the right picture, at least back to about one second after the big bang', he has pointedly avoided taking a view about the initial one. The steady state theory may be in eclipse, but many continue to accept Einstein's view that time is unbounded and space curves in on itself without presenting an edge.

What in any case remains true is that modern cosmology embodies our most extended awareness of the dimensions in which we have our being. Apart from expanding our apprehension of time and space modern science has at the same time revealed the uniformity of nature.[9] Even the most distant stars and galaxies observed by astronomers appear to obey the same laws. Galaxies millions of light years distant not only look like our own but the spectra of their atoms and hence their chemistry and atomic physics appear to be the same. The composition of remote stars resembles that of our own planet. The same uniformity applies to the most minute components of matter. During the present century atoms have been shown to resemble miniature solar systems with electrons orbiting nuclei. The elements hydrogen, carbon, nitrogen and oxygen are not only the commonest in the universe, they also compose 99 per cent of living matter. Moreover, as Donald Goldsmith has pointed out, there is a fundamental unity in the biological world in the sense that all organisms contain the same amino acids, the same proteins and the same DNA and RNA. Although he argues that this suggests a common origin by natural processes, he has to admit that precisely how atoms and molecules combined to form living matter remains unanswered.

This has not prevented the appearance of the nascent science of exobiology,[10] concerned with the study of life beyond the earth. If life in fact developed naturally from the fallout of materials emanating from the stars, it might seem improbable from a purely scientific point of view that it would be confined to a single planet of a star which might not seem of any particular note. Although, as Davies has drily noted,[5] up to the present exobiology 'has no subject matter but plenty of theory', this has not prevented it from being the subject of obsessive speculation ·

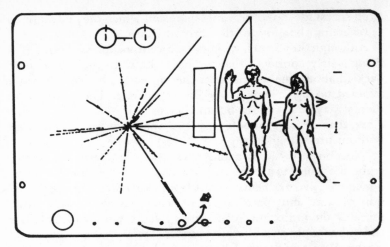

Figure 48 Engraving attached to *Pioneer* spacecraft, providing clues as to who launched the craft and as to the location of the earth. This was intended to be read by the 'scientifically educated inhabitants of some other star system' but, as E. H. Gombrich wrote, 'the directional arrowhead on the trajectory of the spacecraft from the earth swinging past Jupiter could only be understood by people acquainted with the bow and arrow'. ('Visual images', *Scientific American*, September 1973, 82–96)

and even of a certain amount of lobbying. Basing themselves on the universe as perceived by physics, well-qualified authors have come up with suggestions that beggar science fiction. For instance Carl Sagan and Frank Drake, both Professors of Astronomy at Cornell, estimated in 1975 that there should be 'a million civilizations in our galaxy at or beyond the earth's present level of technological development'. The advantage of being able to tap civilizations far in advance of our own is axiomatic. If only we were prepared to put up the 10 billion dollars required, it should be possible, they assure us, even with the telescopes and computers available, to listen in on communications between extraterrestrial civilizations and in this way to draw upon intelligence far ahead of that available on earth. In the meantime efforts have already been made to transmit messages from earth to outer space. The spacecraft Pioneer I and II dispatched in 1973–4 carry with them engraved plaques of gold-anodized aluminium. The symbols engraved on them, destined to be the longest living man-made artefacts and designed to last unchanged for hundreds of millions of years, perhaps a billion years in space, carry outlines of a man and a woman endowed as far as possible with pan-racial characteristics (Figure 48). To establish two-way communication with any intelligences out there would not only be expensive, it would also call for patience well beyond anything yet displayed by human beings. Even if we assume that extraterrestrial civilizations not only exist but are randomly spread, it would take at least 300 years to establish even a one-way traffic. To an archaeologist accustomed by his profession to rely on tangible evidence, the fact that modern reconnaissance of the solar system has failed to disclose any trace of life beyond that known in living or fossil form here on earth may incline him to discount the millions of civilizations envisaged by exobiologists at least until such time as contact is made with any one of them.

# 8

# *Epilogue*

The globe of this earth is evidently made for man. He alone of all
the beings which have life upon this body, enjoys the whole and
every part; he alone is capable of knowing the nature of this
world, which he thus possesses in virtue of his proper right . . .
JAMES HUTTON, 1788

Intelligent life is such a remarkable phenomenon to emerge out
of the basic physical laws that some connection seems implied,
i.e., some correlations between laws and the consequences of the
law – what in common terms we would call a *plan*.
FRED HOYLE, 1965

I began this book by stating that all animals, including man, have
prospered to the extent that they have exploited successfully the
spatial and temporal dimensions of their environments. From
there I went on to claim that one of the most important ways in
which human beings have established their distinct status among
the primates has been by perceiving these dimensions more
consciously and freeing themselves from the constrictions of
confined space and present time. It has been by extending their
perception of space over wider territories and by taking account
of longer periods of time that men have, more than in any other
way, established their unique identity as human beings. They
have done so by inheriting and enlarging their conscious grasp of
the framework of their existence. This has been illustrated in
part by comparing the lives of relatively primitive human
societies with those of non-human primates and in part by
contrasting the perceptions of societies at different stages of
technological development. Until quite recent times people have
only been aware of dimensions immediately relevant to their
way of life. So long as they lived in small communities organized
on a family and clan basis they needed to be aware of only

142

restricted areas of space and of a range of time within the scope of family memory.

It was only as people came to live in more extensive and more highly integrated communities that they experienced the need to take account of wider spaces and lengthier periods of time. The attainment of literacy marked an important stage in the development of the capacity for abstract thought, a development which first appeared in narrowly delimited areas of North Africa and south-west Asia some 5,000 years ago and which has only reached much of the world in modern times. One of the prime topics to engage the attention of the earliest writers and thinkers was to explain how human beings and the world in which they lived had come into existence. The Hebrew account embodied in the Old Testament, which formed an important part of the intellectual heritage of the Europeans who created modern science, described how the earth and its inhabitants, culminating in the appearance of mankind, had come into existence. By taking the text of the scriptures literally and totting up the ages of individuals featured in it, Archbishop Ussher concluded that the world had been created in the year 4004 before the birth of Christ and it was this figure that confronted the early scientists when they sought to date the genesis and geological history of the earth and of the successive forms of life it supported.

The dawn of the modern age in Europe, the heartland of modern science, was marked above all by the world-wide expansion of geographical knowledge and by a radical change in the understanding both of the natural world and of the history of its human inhabitants. Instead of relying on traditional authorities like the Bible, scientists increasingly sought to account for what they experienced in terms of natural processes that were still active and open to observation. In this way the foundations of geology were laid in the final years of eighteenth and the opening half of the nineteenth centuries, a development that enlarged people's perception of time to include the shaping of the earth and the sequence of fossils contained in the succession of rocks accumulated in the course of its history. At the same time biologists sought to account for the sequence of fossils and for the immense variety of living animals and plants as an outcome of natural processes. Their endeavours came to fruition in the publication of Darwin's *Origin of Species*. One reason why the idea of biological evolution met with so much opposition when it was first canvassed is that, like geology, it called for far more time than biblical tradition allowed. Another and probably more important reason is that by invoking natural processes scientists appeared to be making divine intervention increasingly redundant. If this applied to the history of the earth and of biological species in general, it appeared to do so even more in respect of the emergence of more advanced types of hominids, including man, from more primitive ones, a point triumphantly raised by T. H. Huxley in the immediate aftermath of Darwin's book.

If human palaeontology revealed links between the existing and fossil races of man and their pre-human forebears, the application of archaeology to the preliterate phases of mankind has documented an evolutionary development of material culture extending over some 2 million years. At the same time it has disclosed that an important threshold was passed in respect both of physical character and culture within the last 100,000 if not indeed in the last 30,000 years. The appearance of *Homo sapiens sapiens* was marked by the expansion of human settlement beyond the frost-free zone, most notably in northern Eurasia, by the manufacture of a wide variety of comparatively localized styles of artefact adapted in many cases to relatively specialized functions, by notable advances in cognition, including the appearance of art and symbolization, which must have been associated with an advance in articulate speech, and, not least, by the practice of purposive burial of a kind that implies a significant increase in the awareness of time.

An even more dramatic expansion in the apprehension of space and time came with the exploration from the seventeenth century onwards of progressively more extensive tracts of the universe by means of astronomy and the shaping in our own times of modern cosmology. As a result, we have in our own day come to envisage the whole range of time back to the first second following the big bang, and extending outwards towards the edge of outer space. The vast scale of the physical universe, which we know to have been billions of years older than life, and the minimal scale of the human phenomenon have led some physicists, as we saw in the last chapter, to treat the appearance of human beings as an accident that must have been frequently repeated in different parts of the universe. Yet it is important to realize that this view is not shared by all physicists. Certainly it is not entertained by the general run of biologists. Charles Darwin for one never doubted that the evolutionary sequence was crowned by man.

When Darwin went up to Christ's College as an under-graduate, one of the set books he had to master was William Paley's *View of the Evidences of Christianity*, published in 1794, the aim of which was to show that the natural world was created for the benefit of man. Ironically, it was his own work as a biologist that was to dispose of Paley's teleology by showing that man had emerged as victor in a pitiless struggle for biological survival. Man survived because he was best fitted to do so in competition with other organisms in the ordinary course of nature. Those who espouse the modern anthropic principle nevertheless argue that the universe basically favoured his appearance. To make only one elementary point, the very possibility of life as we know it depends on the availability of carbon, hydrogen and oxygen. This alone required a cosmic depth of time. None of these elements was present in the primeval universe. All first appeared in any abundance as an outcome of nucleo-synthesis occurring inside stars. It was only as stars exploded on death that these vital elements became available for building life. In other words, life could only have occurred at a relatively advanced stage in the evolution of the universe. Stars, after all, did not die until they had passed through earlier phases in their develop-ment. Again, the earth itself, the only part of the universe known to have supported life, came into existence only 4.6 billion years ago, that is relatively recently in the time since the universe had been initiated with the big bang. Without going into more detail, we may be sure that if we are to account for the universe and the development of intelligent life by means of natural processes, this in itself necessitates the immense scale of the universe disclosed by modern science.

In summary, it is at least as reasonable to suppose that the emergence of intelligence capable of envisaging the evolution of the universe is indeed the purpose of the whole phenomenon, as to assume that human beings are no more than accidental episodes in the unfolding of physical laws. In his autobiographi-cal writings Charles Darwin tells us that he lost his religious faith at the same time as his pleasure in music and pictures and his capacity even to endure the reading of poetry. Even so, he went on to inform us, he found it extremely difficult, if not impossible, to conceive of 'the immense and wonderful universe, including man with his capacity for looking backwards and far into the future, as the result of blind chance or necessity'. While in such a frame of mind he felt qualified 'to be called a theist'.

In contemplating ourselves an ultimate mystery remains. The second law of thermodynamics assures us that physical systems are subject to degradation in the course of time. The declining rate of expansion recently observed by astrophysicists in respect of the universe suggests that the terminal process may already have begun. Yet if the universe is heading for a singular end, the obverse of the big bang that according to many astrophysicists brought it into being, the question of when this is likely to occur is hardly one to be answered by physics. It remains a mystery as impenetrable by human reason as the origins of the universe or the evolution of beings capable of measuring the dimensions of time and space and even of asking themselves why they exist. As the eminent mathematician and philosopher A. N. Whitehead once put it, 'The present type of order in the world has arisen from an unimaginable past and it will find its grave in an unimaginable future'.[2]

# Notes

## Preface

1 E. Cassirer, *Essay on Man* (New Haven, Yale University Press, 1962).
2 Samuel Alexander, *Space, Time and Deity* (Gifford Lectures, Glasgow, 1927).
3 Grahame Clark, *Aspects of Prehistory* (Berkeley, University of California Press, 1970).
4 Stephen Toulmin and June Goodfield, *The Discovery of Time* (London, Hutchinson, 1965).
5 Geoff Bailey, 'Breaking the time barrier', *Archaeological Review from Cambridge* 1 (1987), 5–10.

## 1 From animal ecology to human history

1 Lord W. R. Brain, *Science and Man* (London, Faber and Faber, 1966).
2 W. H. Thorpe, *Animal Nature and Human Nature* (London, Methuen, 1974).
3 L. and M. Milne, *The Senses of Animals and Men* (London, André Deutsch, 1963).
4 Hans Kummer, *Primate Societies: Group Techniques of Ecological Adaptation* (Chicago, Aldine Atherton, 1971).
5 Adolph H. Schultz, *The Life of the Primates* (London, Weidenfeld and Nicolson, 1969).
6 W. Köhler, *The Mentality of Apes* (London, Kegan Paul, Trench and Trubner, 1969).
7 G. Viaud, *Intelligence: Its Evolution and Forms* (London, Arrow Books, 1960).
8 J. F. Eisenberg and Wilton S. Dillon (eds.), *Man and Beast: Comparative Social Behaviour* (Smithsonian Symposium, 1969; Washington, Smithsonian Institution, 1971).
9 E. Durkheim, *The Elementary Forms of the Religious Life*, 2nd edn (London, Allen and Unwin, 1976).

## 2 Space in preliterate societies

1 Grahame Clark, *World Prehistory in New Perspective* (Cambridge, Cambridge University Press, 1977).
2 C. B. M. McBurney, *Early Man in the Soviet Union* (London, British Academy, 1975); Alexander Mongait, *Archaeology in the USSR* (Moscow, Academy of Sciences, 1959).
3 Grahame Clark, *The Earlier Stone Age Settlement of Scandinavia* (Cambridge, Cambridge University Press, 1975).
4 John Mulvaney, *The Prehistory of Australia* (London, Thames and Hudson, 1969).
5 Peter White and James F. O'Connell, *A Prehistory of Australia, New Guinea and Sahul* (Sydney, Academic Press, 1982).
6 Glyn Daniel, *The Megalith Builders of Western Europe* (London, Hutchinson, 1958).
7 Keith Muckelroy, 'Middle Bronze Age trade between Britain and Europe: a maritime perspective', *Proceedings of the Prehistoric Society* 47 (1981), 275–97.
8 E. V. Wright and D. M. Churchill, 'The boats from North Ferriby, Yorkshire, England, with a review of the origins of sewn boats of the Bronze Age', *Proceedings of the Prehistoric Society* 31 (1965), 1–24.
9 Paul Johnstone, *The Sea-craft of Prehistory* (London, Routledge, 1988).
10 J. C. Beaglehole, *The Exploration of the Pacific*, 3rd edn (London, Blacks, 1966).
11 Peter Bellwood, *The Polynesians: Prehistory of an Island People*, rev. edn (London, Thames and Hudson, 1987).
12 D. Lewis, 'Voyaging stars: aspects of Polynesian and Micronesian astronomy', *Philosophical Transactions of the Royal Society of London* A276 (1974), 113–48.
13 Gwyn Jones, *A History of the Vikings*, 2nd edn (Oxford, Oxford University Press, 1985).
14 J.-M. Geneste, 'Systèmes d'approvisionnement en matières premières au paléolithique moyen et au paléolithique supérieur en Aquitaine', in M. Otte (ed.), *L'Homme de Néandertal 8* (Liège, University of Liège, 1988), pp. 61–70.
15 Gerd C. Weniger, 'Magdalenian settlement and subsistence in south-west Germany', *Proceedings of the Prehistoric Society* 53 (1987), 239–308.
16 Colin Renfrew, J. E. Dixon and J. R. Cann, 'Obsidian and early cultural contact in the Near East', *Proceedings of the Prehistoric Society* 32 (1966), 30–72.
17 Grahame Clark, 'Traffic in stone axe and adze blades', *Economic History Review* 18 (1965), 1–28.

18 Diamond Jenness, *The Indians of Canada* (National Museum of Canada Bulletin 65, Anthropological Series 15, 1955).
19 M. J. Meggitt, *Desert People: A Study of the Walbiri Aborigines of Central Australia* (Sydney, Angus and Robertson, 1962).
20 E. Evans-Pritchard, *The Nuer* (Oxford, Oxford University Press, 1940), chapter 3.
21 Andrew Fleming, 'Co-axial field systems: some questions of time and space', *Antiquity* 61 (1987), 188–202.
22 J. G. D. Clark, 'The archaeology of Stone Age settlement', *Ulster Journal of Archaeology* 35 (1972), 3–16.

## 3 Time in preliterate societies

1 Emile Durkheim, *The Elementary Forms of the Religious Life* (London, Allen and Unwin, 1976), p. 421.
2 D. Black *et al.*, 'Choukoutien cave deposits', *Memoirs of the Geological Survey of China* Series A, no. 11 (1933).
3 T. D. McCown and Sir Arthur Keith, *The Stone Age of Mount Carmel* (Oxford, Oxford University Press, 1939), vol. 2.
4 R. S. Solecki, 'Shanidar Cave, a Palaeolithic site in northern Iraq', *Reports of the Smithsonian Institution* (1954), 389–425.
5 J. G. Frazer, 'Some primitive theories of the origin of man', in A. C. Seward (ed.), *Darwin and Modern Science* (Cambridge, Cambridge University Press, 1907), pp. 152–70.
6 W. Baldwin Spencer and F. J. Gillen, *Native Tribes of Central Australia* (London, Macmillan, 1899).
7 Evans-Pritchard, *The Nuer*.
8 Meyer Fortes, *Oedipus and Job in West African Religion* (Cambridge, Cambridge University Press, 1959).
9 S. Percy Smith, *The Lore of the Whare Wanamga, Part 2* (Wellington, Polynesian Society Memoirs 4, 1915).
10 A. F. Wagner, *English Ancestry* (Oxford, Oxford University Press, 1961).
11 E. R. Leach, 'Primitive time-reckoning', in Charles Singer *et al.* (eds.), *A History of Technology* (Oxford, Oxford University Press, 1954), pp. 110–27.
12 I. Schapera, *The Khoisan Peoples of South Africa* (London, Routledge, 1930).
13 Donald F. Thomson, 'The seasonal factor in human culture', *Proceedings of the Prehistoric Society* 5 (1939), 209–21.
14 W. D. and R. S. Wallis, *The Micmac Indians of Eastern Canada* (Minneapolis, University of Minnesota Press, 1955).
15 Raymond Firth, *We, the Tikopia* (London, George Allen and Unwin, 1936).

16  Leo Austin, 'The seasonal gardening calendar of Kiriwina, Trobriand Islands', *Oceania* 9 (1939), 237–53.
17  M. L. West (ed.), Hesiod's *Works and Days* (Oxford, Clarendon Press, 1978).
18  Sylvanus G. Morley and George W. Brainerd, *The Ancient Maya*, 3rd edn (Stanford, Stanford University Press, 1956): Anthony F. Aveni (ed.), *Native American Astronomy* (Austin, University of Texas Press, 1972.
19  R. J. C. Atkinson, *Stonehenge* (London, Hamish Hamilton, 1956).
20  Gerald S. Hawkins, *Stonehenge Decoded* (New York, Delta Books, 1965).
21  A. and S. Thom, *Megalithic Remains in Britain and Brittany* (Oxford, Clarendon Press, 1978).
22  A. Marshack, *The Roots of Civilization* (London, Weidenfeld and Nicolson, 1972).
23  Daniel, *The Megalith Builders.*
24  McBurney, *Early Man in the Soviet Union.*
25  Jorg Biel, 'A Celtic grave in Hochdorf, Germany', *Archaeology* (1987), 22–9.
26  R. Bruce-Mitford, *The Sutton Hoo Ship Burial* (3 vols., London, British Museum Publications, 1975–83).

## 4  *Civilization and the expansion of space*

1  T. G. H. James, *An Introduction to Ancient Egypt* (London, British Museum Publications, 1979), chapters 1 and 2.
2  Paul Lipke, *The Royal Ship of Cheops* (Oxford, British Archaeological Reports, International Series 225/ Green wich, National Maritime Museum Archaeological Series 9, 1984).
3  Mortimer Wheeler, *The Indus Civilization*, 3rd edn (Cambridge, Cambridge University Press, 1968).
4  Lord William Taylour, *The Mycenaeans* (London, Thames and Hudson, 1964).
5  Michael Grant, *Ancient History Atlas* (London, Weidenfeld and Nicolson, 1971).
6  Donald Harden, *The Phoenicians* (London, Thames and Hudson, 1962).
7  Lionel Casson, *Travel in the Ancient World* (London, Allen and Unwin, 1974).
8  Peter Salway, *Roman Britain* (Oxford, Oxford University Press, 1981).
9  Eric Birley, *Vindolanda* (London, Thames and Hudson, 1977), chapter 8.

10 D. A. W. Dilke, *Greek and Roman Maps* (London, Thames and Hudson, 1985).
11 Bulling A. Gutkind, 'Ancient Chinese maps: two maps discovered in a Han Dynasty tomb from the second century B.C.', *Expedition* (1978), 16–25.
12 Marco Polo, *The Travels of Marco Polo the Venetian*, trans. and revised by T. Wright (London, Dent, 1926).
13 Geoffrey Bushnell, *Peru* (London, Thames and Hudson, 1956).
14 Victor W. von Hagen, *The Ancient Sun Kingdoms of the Americas* (London, Thames and Hudson, 1962), chapter 18.
15 J. H. Parry, *The Age of Reconnaissance* (London, Weidenfeld and Nicolson, 1963).
16 Ferdinand Magellan, *The First Voyage round the World by Magellan*, trans. by Lord Stanley of Alderley (Hakluyt Society 52, 1874).
17 G. R. Crone, *Maps and their Makers: An Introduction to the History of Cartography*, 4th edn (London, Hutchinson, 1968). For a much fuller and more recent treatment the reader is referred to J. B. Hartley and David Woodward (eds.), *The History of Cartography I: Cartography in Prehistoric, Ancient, and Medieval Europe and the Mediterranean* (Chicago, University of Chicago Press, 1987).
18 G. R. Crone, *Modern Geographers: An Outline of Progress in Geography since A.D. 1800* (London, Hamish Hamilton, 1970).

## 5 Civilization and the deepening of historical time

1 W. C. Hayes, 'Chronology. Egypt – to the end of the Twentieth Dynasty', in *Cambridge Ancient History* (Cambridge, Cambridge University Press, 1970), vol. 1, part 1, pp. 173–93.
2 T. G. H. James, *An Introduction to Ancient Egypt* (London, British Museum Publications, 1979), chapter 2.
3 M. B. Rowton, 'Chronology. Ancient Western Asia', in *Cambridge Ancient History* (Cambridge, Cambridge University Press, 1970), vol. 1, part 1, pp. 193–239.
4 Seton Lloyd, *Twin Rivers* (Oxford, Oxford University Press, 1943), chapter 2.
5 H. W. F. Saggs, *The Encounter with the Divine in Mesopotamia and Israel* (London, Athlone Press, 1978).
6 C. P. Fitzgerald, *China: A Short Cultural History* (London, Cresset Press, 1965).
7 Joseph Needham, *Science and Civilization in China* (Cambridge, Cambridge University Press, 1965), vol. 1.
8 Michael Sullivan, *A Short History of Chinese Art* (London, Faber and Faber, 1967).

9 David N. Keightley, *Sources of Shang History: The Oracle-bone Inscriptions of Bronze Age China* (Berkeley, University of California Press, 1978).

10 M. I. Finley, *Ancient Culture and Society: Early Greece: The Bronze and Archaic Ages* (London, Chatto and Windus, 1977).

11 J. B. Bury, *The Ancient Greek Historians* (London, Macmillan, 1939).

12 Herbert Butterfield, *Man on his Past* (Cambridge, Cambridge University Press, 1954).

13 Jack Goody, 'The social organisation of time', in *International Encyclopaedia of the Social Sciences* (New York, Macmillan, 1930), vol. 16, pp. 30–42.

14 Lynn White, *Medieval Technology and Social Change* (Oxford, Oxford University Press, 1962).

## 6 *Evolution and world prehistory*

1 Frazer, 'Some primitive theories'.

2 James Ussher, Archbishop of Armagh, *The Annals of the World* (London, 1658).

3 J. B. Bury, 'Darwinism and history', in A. C. Seward (ed.), *Darwin and Modern Science* (Cambridge, Cambridge University Press, 1907), p. 529.

4 F. C. Haber, *The Age of the World, Moses to Darwin* (Baltimore, Johns Hopkins University Press, 1959).

5 Gavin de Beer (ed.), *Charles Darwin and Henry Huxley Autobiographies* (Oxford, Oxford University Press, 1974).

6 Charles Lyell, *Principles of Geology* (London, J. Murray, 1830–3).

7 Jean Priveteau, *Traités de paléontologie* (Paris, Masson, 1952).

8 Archibald Geikie, *The Founders of Geology* (London, Macmillan, 1905).

9 George W. White (ed.), *Contributions to the History of Geology* (Darien, Conn., Hafner, 1907), vol. 5.

10 Thomas H. Huxley, *Evidence as to Man's Place in Nature* (London, Williams and Norgate, 1863).

11 L. R. Wager, 'The history of attempts to establish a quantitative time-scale', *Quarterly Journal of the Geological Society of London* 120 (1964), 13–28.

12 W. B. Harland *et al.* (eds.), *The Phanerozoic Time-scale: A Symposium Dedicated to Professor Arthur Holmes* (London, *Quarterly Journal of the Geological Society of London*, supplement to vol. 120, 1964).

13 H. R. von Koenigswald, *Hundert Jahre Neandertaler* (Cologne, Böhlau-Verlag, 1958).

14 Kenneth Oakley, *Frameworks for Dating Fossil Man* (London, Weidenfeld and Nicolson, 1964).

15 Glynn Ll. Isaac and Elizabeth R. McCown (eds.), *Human Origins: Louis Leakey and the East African Evidence* (Menlow Park, Calif., W. A. Benjamin, 1976).

16 R. Foley, 'Hominids, humans and hunter-gatherers: an evolutionary perspective' in T. Ingold *et al.* (eds.), *Hunters and Gatherers. I: History, Evolution and Social Change* (Oxford, Berg, 1982), pp. 201–21.

17 Glyn Daniel, *A Hundred and Fifty Years of Archaeology* (London, Duckworth, 1975).

18 Sir John Lubbock, *Pre-historic Times* (London, Williams and Norgate, 1865).

19 Willard F. Libby, *Radiocarbon Dating* (Chicago, University of Chicago Press, 1952).

20 Grahame Clark, 'World prehistory and natural science', *Historisk-Filosofiske Meddelelser* 50 (1980), 1–40.

21 Clark, *World Prehistory*.

22 Mulvaney, *The Prehistory of Australia*.

## 7 Extraterrestrial space and time

1 A. Pannekoek, *A History of Astronomy* (London, Allen and Unwin, 1969).

2 Patrick Moore, *The Story of Astronomy*, 4th edn (London, Macdonald, 1972).

3 D. W. Sciama, *Modern Cosmology* (Cambridge, Cambridge University Press, 1971).

4 P. C. W. Davies, *Space and Time in the Modern Universe* (Cambridge, Cambridge University Press, 1977).

5 P. C. W. Davies, *The Accidental Universe* (Cambridge, Cambridge University Press, 1982).

6 Donald Goldsmith, *The Evolving Universe* (Menlow, Calif., Benjamin/Cummins, 1981).

7 Stephen Hawking, *A Brief History of Time from the Big Bang to Black Holes* (London, Bantam Press, 1988).

8 David O. Edge and Michael J. Mulkay, *Astronomy Transformed: The Emergence of Radio Astronomy in Britain* (New York, Wiley, 1978).

9 D. W. Sciama, *The Unity of the Universe* (London, Faber and Faber, 1959).

10 Carl Sagan and Frank Drake, 'The search for extraterrestrial intelligence', *Scientific American* 232 (May 1975), 80–9.

## 8 *Epilogue*

1 Fred Hoyle, *Of Men and Galaxies* (London, Heinemann, 1965).
2 A. N. Whitehead, *Religion in the Making* (Cambridge, Cambridge University Press, 1928).

# Bibliography

Atkinson, R. J. C., *Stonehenge*. London, Hamish Hamilton, 1956.

Austin, Leo, 'The seasonal gardening calendar of Kiriwina, Trobiand Islands', *Oceania* 9 (1939), 237–53.

Aveni, Anthony F. (ed.), *Native American Astronomy*. Austin, University of Texas Press, 1972.

Baldwin, Spencer W. and F. J. Gillen, *Native Tribes of Central Australia*. London, Macmillan, 1899.

Barrow, John D. and Frank J. Tipler, *The Anthropic Cosmological Principle*. Oxford, Clarendon Press, 1966.

Beaglehole, J. C., *The Exploration of the Pacific*, 3rd edn. London, Blacks, 1966.

Bellwood, Peter, *The Polynesians: Prehistory of an Island People*, rev. edn. London, Thames and Hudson, 1987.

Bengtson, Hermann and Vladimir Milojcic (eds.), *Grosser Historischer Weltatlas. Teil I. Vorgeschichte und Altertum*. Munich, Bayerischer Schulbuch-Verlag, 1953.

Biel, Jorg, 'A Celtic grave in Hochdorf, Germany', *Archaeology* (Nov./Dec. 1987), 22–9.

Birley, Eric, *Vindolanda*. London, Thames and Hudson, 1977.

Black, D., P. Teilhard de Chardin, C. C. Young and W. C. Pei, 'The Chou Koutien cave deposits', *Memoirs of the Geological Survey of China*, Series A, no. 11, 1933.

Brain, Lord W. R., *Science and Man*. London, Faber and Faber, 1966.

Bruce-Mitford, R., *The Sutton Hoo Ship Burial*, 3 vols. London, British Museum Publications, 1975–83.

Bury, J. B., 'Darwinism and history'. *Darwin and Modern Science* (ed. A. C. Seward), pp. 529–42. Cambridge, Cambridge University Press, 1907.

　*The Ancient Greek Historians*. London, Macmillan, 1939.

Bushnell, Geoffrey, *Peru*. London, Thames and Hudson, 1956.

Butterfield, Herbert, *Man on his Past*. Cambridge, Cambridge University Press, 1954.

Casson, Lionel, *Ships and Seamanship in the Ancient World*. Princeton, Princeton University Press, 1971.

*Travel in the Ancient World*. London, Allen and Unwin, 1974.

Clark, Grahame, 'Traffic in stone axe and adze blades', *Economic History Review* 18 (1965), 1–28.

'The archaeology of Stone Age settlement', *Ulster Journal of Archaeology* 35 (1972), 3–16.

*The Earlier Stone Age Settlement of Scandinavia*. Cambridge, Cambridge University Press, 1975.

*World Prehistory*. Cambridge, Cambridge University Press: 1st edn. 1961; 2nd edn 1969; 3rd edn 1977.

*World Prehistory in New Perspective*. Cambridge, Cambridge University Press, 1977.

'World prehistory and natural science', *Historisk-filosofiske Meddelelser* 50 (1980), 1–40.

Crone, G. R., *Maps and their Makers. An Introduction to the History of Cartography*, 4th edn. London, Hutchinson, 1968.

*Modern Geographers: An Outline of Progress in geography since AD 1800*. London, Hamish Hamilton, 1969.

Daniel, Glyn, *A Hundred and Fifty Years of Archaeology*, London, Duckworth, 1975.

*The Megalith Builders of Western Europe*. London, Hutchinson, 1958.

Davies, P. C. W., *Space and Time in the Modern Universe*. Cambridge, Cambridge University Press, 1977.

*The Accidental Universe*. Cambridge, Cambridge University Press, 1982.

De Beer, Gavin (ed.), *Charles Darwin and Henry Huxley Autobiographies*. Oxford, Oxford University Press, 1974.

Dilke, D. A. W., *Greek and Roman Maps*. London, Thames and Hudson, 1985.

Durkheim, E., *The Elementary Forms of the Religious Life*, 2nd edn. London, Allen and Unwin, 1976.

Edge, David O. and Michael J. Mulkay, *Astronomy Transformed: The Emergence of Radio Astronomy in Britain*. New York, John Wiley and Sons, 1978.

Eisenberg, J. F. and Wilton S. Dillon (eds.), *Man and Beast: Comparative Social Behaviour*. Smithsonian Symposium, 1969. Washington, Smithsonian Institution, 1971.

Evans-Pritchard, E., *The Nuer*. Oxford, Oxford University Press, 1940.

Everidden, J. F. and C. H. Curtis, 'The potassium argon dating of the late Cenozoic rocks in East Africa and Italy', *Current Anthropology* 6 (1965), 343–85.

Finley, M. I., *Ancient Culture and Society: Early Greece: The Bronze and Archaic Ages*. London, Chatto and Windus, 1977.

Firth, Raymond, *We, the Tikopia*. London, Allen and Unwin, 1936.

Fitzgerald, C. P., *China: A Short Cultural History*. London, Cresset Press, 1965.

Fleming, Andrew, 'Co-axial field systems: some questions of time and space', *Antiquity* 61 (1987), 188–202.

Flint, R. F., *Glacial and Quaternary Geology*, 3rd edn. New York, John Wiley and Sons, 1971.

Foley, R., 'Hominids, humans and hunter-gatherers: an evolutionary perspective'. *Hunters and Gatherers I: History, Evolution and Social Change* (ed. T. Ingold, D. Riches and J. Woodhead), pp. 207–21. Explorations in Anthropology, University College London. Oxford, Berg, 1982.

Fortes, Meyer, *Oedipus and Job in West African Religion*. Cambridge, Cambridge University Press, 1959.

Fox, Cyril, *The Archaeology of the Cambridge Region*. Cambridge, Cambridge University Press, 1923.

Frazer, J. G., 'Some primitive theories of the origin of man'. *Darwin and Modern Science* (ed. A. C. Steward), pp. 152–70. Cambridge, Cambridge University Press, 1907.

Geikie, Archibald, *The Founders of Geology*. London, Macmillan, 1905.

Geneste, J.-M., 'Systèmes d'approvisionnement en matières premières au paléolithique moyen et au paléolithique supérieur en Aquitaine'. *L'Homme de Néandertal 8* (ed. M. Otte), pp. 61–70. Liège, 1988.

Goldsmith, Donald, *The Evolving Universe*. Menlo, Calif., Benjamin/Cummins, 1981.

Goody, Jack, 'The social organisation of time'. *International Encyclopaedia of the Social Sciences*, vol. 16, pp. 30–42. New York: Macmillan, 1930.

Gould, Richard A., *Yiwara: Foragers of the Australian Desert*. London, Collins, 1969.

Grant, Michael, *Ancient History Atlas*. London, Weidenfeld and Nicolson, 1971.

Grimes, W. F., 'The Jurassic Way'. *Aspects of Archaeology in Britain and Beyond* (ed. W. F. Grimes), pp. 144–71. London, H. W. Edwards, 1951.

Gutkind, Bulling A., 'Ancient Chinese maps: two maps discovered in a Han Dynasty tomb from the second century B.C.', *Expedition* (1978), 16–25.

Haber, F. C., *The Age of the World, Moses to Darwin*. Baltimore, Johns Hopkins University Press, 1959.

Harden, Donald, *The Phoenicians*. London, Thames and Hudson, 1962.

Harland, W. B. *et al.* (eds.), *The Phanerozoic Time-scale: A Symposium Dedicated to Professor Arthur Holmes*. Supplement to vol. 120, *Quarterly Journal of the Geological Society of London*, 1964.

Hawking, Stephen, *A Brief History of Time from the Big Bang to Black Holes*. London, Bantam Press, 1988.

Hawkins, Gerald S., *Stonehenge Decoded*. New York, Delta Books, 1965.

Hayes, W. C., 'Chronology: Egypt – to the end of the Twentieth Dynasty'. *Cambridge Ancient History*, vol. 1, part 1, chap. 6, pp. 173–93. Cambridge, Cambridge University Press, 1970.

Hoyle, Fred, *Of Men and Galaxies* (John Danz Lectures, University of Michigan). London, Heinemann, 1965.

Hutton, James, *see* George W. White (ed.).

Huxley, Thomas H., *Evidence as to Man's Place in Nature*, London, Williams and Norgate, 1863.

Isaac, Glynn Ll. and Elizabeth R. McCown (eds.), *Human Origins: Louis Leakey and the East African Evidence*. Menlow Park, Calif., W. A. Benjamin, 1976.

James, T. G. H., *An Introduction to Ancient Egypt*. London, British Museum Publications, 1979.

Jenness, Diamond, *The Indians of Canada*. National Museum of Canada, Bulletin 65, Anthropological Series 15, 1955.

Johnstone, Paul, *The Sea-craft of Prehistory*. London, Routledge, 1988.

Jones, Gwyn, *A History of the Vikings*, 2nd edn. Oxford, Oxford University Press, 1985.

Keightley, David N., *Sources of Shang History: The Oracle – Inscriptions of Bronze Age China*. University of California Press, Berkeley, 1978.

Köhler, W., *The Mentality of Apes*. London, Kegan Paul, Trench and Trubner, 1969.

Kummer, Hans, *Primate Societies: Group Techniques of Ecological Adaptation*. Chicago, Aldine Atherton, 1971.

Leach, E. R., 'Primitive calendars', *Oceania* 20 (1950), 245–62.
'Primitive time-reckoning', chap. 5, *A History of Technology* (ed. Charles Singer *et al.*) Oxford, Oxford University Press, 1954.

Lewis, D., 'Voyaging stars: aspects of Polynesian and Micronesian astronomy', *Philosophical Transactions of the Royal Society of London*, A276 (1974), 133–48.

Lewis, Richard S., *Space Exploration*. London, Salamander Books, 1983.

Libby, Willard F., *Radiocarbon Dating*. Chicago, University of Chicago Press, 1952.

Lipke, Paul, *The Royal Ship of Cheops*. National Maritime Museum, Greenwich, Archaeological Series no. 9. Oxford, BAR International Series 225, 1984.

Lloyd, Seton, *Twin Rivers*, chap. 2. Oxford, Oxford University Press, 1943.

Lubbock, Sir John, *Prehistoric Times*. London, Williams and Norgate, 1865.

Lyell, Charles, *Principles of Geology*. London, J. Murray, 1830–3.

McBurney, C. B. M., *Early Man in the Soviet Union*. London, British Academy, 1975.

McCown, T. D. and Sir Arthur Keith, *The Stone Age of Mount Carmel*, vol. 2. Oxford, Oxford University Press, 1939.

Magellan, Ferdinand, *The First Voyage Round the World by Magellan*, trans. Lord Stanley of Alderley. Hakluyt Society 52, 1874.

Mallowan, Max, *Early Mesopotamia and Iran*. London, Thames and Hudson, 1965.

Marshack, A., *The Roots of Civilization*. London, Weidenfeld and Nicolson, 1972.

Meggitt, M. J., *Desert People: A Study of the Walbiri Aborigines of Central Australia*. Sydney, Angus and Robertson, 1962.

Milne, L. and M., *The Senses of Animals and Men*. London, André Deutsch, 1963.

Mongait, Alexander, *Archaeology in the USSR*. Moscow, Academy of Sciences, 1959.

Moore, Patrick, *The Story of Astronomy*, 4th edn. London, Macdonald, 1972.

Morley, Sylvanus G. and George W. Brainerd, *The Ancient Maya*, 3rd edn. Stanford, Stanford University Press, 1956.

Muckelroy, Keith, 'Middle Bronze Age trade between Britain and Europe: a maritime perspective', *Proceedings of the Prehistoric Society* 47 (1981), 275–97.

Mulvaney, D. J., *The Prehistory of Australia*. London, Thames and Hudson, 1969.

Needham, Joseph, *Science and Civilization in China*, vols. 1, part 3 and vol. 4, part 2. Cambridge, Cambridge University Press, 1959 and 1965.

Oakley, Kenneth, *Frameworks for Dating Fossil Man*. London, Weidenfeld and Nicolson, 1964.

Pannekoek, A., *A History of Astronomy*. London, Allen and Unwin, 1969.

Parry, J. H., *The Age of Reconnaissance*. London, Weidenfeld and Nicolson, 1963.

Polo, Marco, *The Travels of Marco Polo the Venetian*, trans. and revised by T. Wright. London, Dent, 1926.

Priveteau, Jean, *Traités de paléontologie*. Paris, Masson, 1952.

Renfrew, Colin, J. E. Dixon and J. R. Cann, 'Obsidian and early cultural contact in the Near East', *Proceedings of the Prehistoric Society* 32 (1966), 30–72.

Rowton, M. B., 'Chronology: ancient western Asia'. *Cambridge Ancient History*, vol. 1, chap. 6, pp. 193–239. Cambridge, Cambridge University Press, 1970.

Sagan, Carl and Frank Drake, 'The search for extraterritorial intelligence', *Scientific American* 232 (May 1975), 80–9.

Saggs, H. W. F., *The Encounter with the Divine in Mesopotamia and Israel*. London, Athlone Press, 1978.

Salway, Peter, *Roman Britain*. Oxford, Oxford University Press, 1984.

Schapera, I., *The Khoisian Peoples of South Africa*. London, Routledge, 1930.

Schultz, Adolph H., *The Life of the Primates*. London, Weidenfeld and Nicolson, 1969.

Sciama, D. W., *The Unity of the Universe*. London, Faber and Faber, 1959. *Modern Cosmology*. Cambridge, Cambridge University Press, 1971.

Smith, Percy S., *The Lore of the Whare Wanamga, Part 2*. Polynesian Society Memoir 4. Wellington, 1915.

Solecki, R. S., 'Shanidar Cave, a Palaeolithic site in north Iraq', *Reports of the Smithsonian Institution*, 1954, pp. 389–425.

Sullivan, Michael, *A Short History of Chinese Art*. London, Faber and Faber, 1967.

Taylour, William Lord, *The Mycenaeans*. London, Thames and Hudson, 1964.

Thom, A. and S., *Megalithic Remains in Britain and Brittany*. Oxford, Clarendon Press, 1978.

Thomson, Donald F., 'The seasonal factor in human culture', *Proceedings of the Prehistoric Society* 5 (1939), 209–21.

Thorpe, W. H., *Animal Nature and Human Nature*. London, Methuen, 1974.

Viaud, G., *Intelligence: Its Evolution and Forms*. London, Arrow Books, 1960.

Von Hagen, Victor, *The Ancient Sun Kingdoms of the Americas*, chap. 18. London, Thames and Hudson, 1962.

Von Koenigswald, G. H. R., *Hundert Jahre Neanderthaler*, Cologne, Böhlau-Verlag, 1958.

Wager, L. R., 'The history of attempts to establish a quantitative time-scale', *Quarterly Journal of the Geological Society of London* 120 (1964), 13–28.

Wagner, A. F., *English Ancestry*. Oxford, Oxford University Press, 1961.

Wallis, W. D. and R. S., *The Micmac Indians of Eastern Canada*, Minneapolis, University of Minnesota Press, 1955.

Weniger, Gerd-C., 'Magdalenian settlement and subsistence in south-east Germany', *Proceedings of the Prehistoric Society* 53 (1987), 293–308.

West, M. L. (ed.), Hesiod's *Works and Days*. Oxford, Clarendon Press, 1978.

Wheeler, Mortimer, *The Indus Civilization*, 3rd edn. Cambridge, Cambridge University Press, 1968.

White, George W. (ed.), *Contributions to the History of Geology*, vol. 5. Darien, Conn., Hafner, 1907.

White, Lynn, *Medieval Technology and Social Change*. Oxford, Oxford University Press, 1962.

White, Peter and James F. O'Connell, *A Prehistory of Australia, New Guinea and Sahul*. Sydney, Academic Press, 1982.

Whitehead, A. N., *Religion in the Making*. Cambridge, Cambridge University Press, 1928.

Wright, E. V. and D. M. Churchill, 'The boats from North Ferriby, Yorkshire, England, with a review of the origins of sewn boats of the Bronze Age', *Proceedings of the Prehistoric Society* 31 (1965), 1–24.

# Index

cursus monuments 33
Cuvier, Georges 109

Dartmoor reaves 33f.
Darwin, Charles 8, 108–12, 135, 143ff.
Davies, P. C. W. 125, 139
death 39ff.
Delphi 97
Diaz, Bartholomew 7
divination 92f., 96f.
Drake, Frank 140
Druids 55
Durkheim, Emile 10, 39

Egypt 24, 60–5, 87–91
Einstein, Albert 139
*Endeavour* 25
Ephimenkoe, P. P. 16
Eratosthenes 67, 126
Eric the Red 27
Eskimo 18f. 29
ethology xii, 1ff., 9f.
Evans-Pritchard, E. xii, 9, 32, 47f.
exchange 22ff., 30f., 36f., *see also* trade
exobiology 139
extraterritorial space 85f.

Finley, Moses 69
Firth, Sir Raymond 47
Fortes, Meyer xii, 42, 56
Fox, Robin 9
Fraser, Sir James 41, 106
Frere, John 120

Gagarin, Yuri 131
galaxies 136ff.
Galilee 127f., 133
Gasset, Ortega y 6
genealogies 42ff.
geography 14–59, 143
geology xii, 12, 109ff., 120, 143
Gibbon, Edward 101
Glenn, John 131
Gombrich, Sir Ernst 140
Goodfield, June xii
Greeks 49f., 65ff., 97ff.
Greenwich Observatory 128

Hadrian's Wall 76
Halley, Edmund 128, 134
Halls, Louis J. 8
Harappan civilization 63f.
Hawking, Stephen 139
Hawkins, Gerald 52f., 55
Herodotus 65, 98
Hershel, William 133f.
Hesiod 49f.
Hipparchus 126
history 11, 87, 93f., 98–102
Hohenasperg 57, 59
Holmes, Arthur 113f.
Homer 97f.
*Homo habilis* 117
*Homo sapiens* xi, 12, 14, 40, 116, 119; *see also* Neanderthal man
Hoxne 120
Hoyle, Sir Fred 135, 142
Hubble, Edwin 135f.
Huelva heard 23
human palaeontology 115ff., 144
Hutton, James 109f., 135, 142
Huxley, T. H. 8, 111ff., 144

Inuit, *see* Eskimo
investment 105
Ireland 27, 77

Kant, Immanuel 134
Kew Gardens 107
Köhler, Wolfgang 6
Kostienki 16

Laetoli 117f.
Lamarck, J. B. 109
Langdon Cliff, Dover 22
Langer, Susanne 8
language, articulate 6, 8, 81
Leach, Sir Edmund xii, 38
Leakey family 117
Lewis, C. S. 127
Libby, Willard 122
Linnaeus, Carolus 107
literacy 10f., 87–91, 119
Livy 99
Lockyer, Sir Norman 53
Lovell, Sir Bernard 138